MARCO ⊕ POLO

Travel with
**Insider
Tips**

KRAKOW

LATVIA

SWEDEN   LITHUANIA

Baltic Sea

RUS

Gdańsk

BELARUS

Szczecin

Berlin   Warsaw

GERMANY   **POLAND**

Wrocław

Krakow   UKRAINE

CZECH REP.   MD

SLOVAKIA

Vienna   ROMANIA

AUSTRIA
HUNGARY

SYMBOLS

INSIDER TIP   Insider Tip

★   Highlight

●●●●   Best of ...

☼   Scenic view

☺   Responsible travel: fair
trade principles and the
environment respected

PRICE CATEGORIES HOTELS

Expensive	over 550 złoty
Moderate	250–550 złoty
Budget	under 250 złoty

The prices are for a double
room per night including
breakfast

PRICE CATEGORIES RESTAURANTS

Expensive	over 75 złoty
Moderate	40–75 złoty
Budget	under 40 złoty

The prices are for a three-
course meal without drinks

On the cover: The 'Underground Museum' p. 34 | The trendy Kazimierz district p. 42

CONTENTS

Shopping → p. 60

Entertainment → p. 66

Where to stay → p. 74

Street atlas → p. 106

DID YOU KNOW?

MAPS IN THE GUIDEBOOK

(108 A1) Page numbers
and coordinates refer to
the street atlas
(0) Site/address located off
the map
Coordinates are also given for
places that are not marked
on the street atlas
A public transportation map
can be found inside the back
cover

**INSIDE BACK COVER:
PULL-OUT MAP →**

PULL-OUT MAP *⫽*

(*⫽ A–B 2–3*) Refers to the
removable pull-out map

The best
MARCO POLO
Insider Tips

Our top 15 Insider Tips

INSIDER TIP Japan in Krakow
Experience all the flair of the Orient during a far-eastern tea ceremony on the terrace of the café in the Manggha Culture Centre with its view of Wawel Hill → S. 54

INSIDER TIP Mother's cooking
No matter whether they are filled with meat, potato, mushrooms or strawberries: countless varieties of *pierogi*, Poland's traditional stuffed dumplings, are waiting to be savoured at Pierożki u Vincenta (photo below) → p. 56

INSIDER TIP Wooden children's world
Ecological, handmade and produced in Krakow in every conceivable size: Bajo sells wonderful wooden toys for children → p. 63

INSIDER TIP The beauty of nature
The striped flint at A&S is rare and quite unique, as is the great variety of imaginative and eye-catching amber jewellery → p. 64

INSIDER TIP Live with the astronomer
The rooms in the Hotel Copernicus with a view of ul. Kanonicza will make you forget the 21st century. It is said that Copernicus himself stayed here → p. 76

INSIDER TIP Otherworldly
Death and art – the exhibition of Baroque funeral customs in the Erazm Ciołek Museum is pleasantly spooky → p. 37

INSIDER TIP The Wawel outside your window
The beautiful panorama rooms in the Hotel Poleski have marvellous views of the hill, castle and river → p. 79

INSIDER TIP Tasty cult snack
It is worth lining up at U Endziora, a snack bar in the Okrąglak on Plac Nowy, to try the delicious *zapiekanka*, a kind of Polish pizza with various toppings on crispy white bread → p. 43

BEST OF ...

GREAT PLACES FOR FREE
Discover new places and save money

● *Visit the oldest synagogue in Poland*
Normally you have to pay to visit the 15th-century *Synagoga Stara* but no admission is charged if you go to the oldest Jewish temple and its museum on Mondays → p. 45

● *A treat for your ears*
Enjoy a concert of classical music in perfect surroundings free of charge: these impressive musical events are held in many *Krakow churches* and you will not have to pay a penny → p. 33

● *History lesson in the Coronation Church*
Wawel Cathedral on Wawel Hill was also the Coronation Church and is one of the most important sights in Poland – nonetheless, no entrance fee is charged to visit the church's elaborately decorated interior (photo) → p. 38

● *Art under a canopy of leaves*
It is hard to imagine a more beautiful site for a sculpture exhibition: Stroll through the *Planty*, the parkland surrounding the Old Town and admire one of the largest collections of monuments from the 19th and 20th centuries → p. 33

● *Feel free to visit the museum on Sunday ...*
No matter whether it is the *Mehoffer House, National Museum* or the *Archaeological Museum on the Wawel:* you can visit many permanent exhibitions on Sunday without having to pay → p. 33

● *Party – without limits*
For all those who want to dance the Krakow night away and have sufficient stamina: most of the clubs do not charge an admission fee after around 1 o'clock in the morning → p. 72

● *Gratis to the Museum of Modern Art*
On Tuesday, you can experience the fascination of modern art for nothing – that is the day the *MOCAK* does not charge an entrance fee. But, come early – the free tickets are in great demand → p. 47

●●●● Dots in guidebook refer to 'Best of ...' tips

● *The dancing, fire-breathing dragon*

The legend lives on: The dragon from the medieval saga can be seen everywhere in the city and is at the heart of the annual *Dragon Parade* in June, a celebration with many concerts and family picnics on the Vistula river → p. 90

● *In the astronomer's study*

Poland's oldest university had already been operating for 130 years when Nicolaus Copernicus started his studies at the *Collegium Maius*. A tour of the spectacular library is like a journey back through time → p. 30

● *In the heart of town*

The *Rynek Główny* is not only the largest Gothic square in Europe but also one of the most beautiful. Climb up the Town Hall Tower and be charmed by the unique expanse and architecture of the Market Square down below → p. 33, 35

● *Hear international jazz musicians live*

Krakow is a jazz city and the stars perform in the fabulous brick-wall setting of an old cellar in *Harris Piano Jazz Bar* – you can recharge your batteries with the good music and drinks served there! (photo) → p. 70

● *Royal carpets that tell a tale*

Monarchs know how to decorate in style: in the *Royal Castle Museum* on Wawel Hill, you can admire the precious tapestries that King Zygmunt August had produced in Brussels in the 16th century → p. 41

● *The sunken world of Medieval Krakow*

You can really delve deep into the history of the city in the *Rynek Podziemny (Underground Museum)*: a mysteriously illuminated, detailed reconstruction of the world of Medieval Krakow awaits visitors beneath the Cloth Hall → p. 34

● *Synagogues and the sound of klezmer*

You will get an intense taste of Jewish history and culture in Kazimierz: in the evening, swinging klezmer music, which combines a large number of individual styles, is served with Jewish food in the *Klezmer Hois* → p. 59

ONLY IN

BEST OF ...

AND IF IT RAINS?
Activities to brighten your day

● **Visit the lady and her pet**
Would you like to see a genuine Leonardo da Vinci? There is one in the *Czartoryski Museum*. The 'Lady with the Ermine' holds court there surrounded by many other priceless artworks from the Middle Ages to well into the 19th century → p. 32

● **A cup of coffee and a book please!**
Drink a cup of coffee, browse through novels and illustrated books, buy and write postcards, visit photo exhibitions, wait for the weather to improve: Welcome to the *Café Bona*! → p. 61

● **Escape to the dream factory**
An excellent way to wait for the rain to stop is in the very special atmosphere of the five charmingly old-fashioned auditoriums with their plush seats and old lamps in the *Ars Cinema Centre*. The cinema café Kiniarnia is also rather enchanting → p. 71

● **Follow the red brick road**
The original brick architecture was integrated into the modern construction of the *Galeria Kazimierz* shopping centre. This special charm, as well as the cinemas, restaurants, cafés and a play area for children, makes this one of the more pleasant places to go shopping → p. 62

● **Through the hard war years**
In Oskar Schindler's former enamelware factory, you will be able to learn about the indescribable suffering experienced by the Jewish and non-Jewish population during the Nazi occupation. You should allow yourself plenty of time for this moving experience → p. 46

● **Monkeys in the Museum of Natural History**
Just what are those monkeys doing between the aquariums with the colourful fish? Find out for yourself in the *Aquarium and Museum of Natural History* with its secret stars: the two cotton-top tamarin monkeys → p. 88

RELAX AND CHILL OUT
Take it easy and spoil yourself

● *Watch the flowers grow*
The *Botanical Gardens* cover an impressive 25 acres. Being able to sit near a small lake on a warm day, read a book or just watch the flowers grow is absolute heaven (photo) → **p. 49**

● *Invigorate weary limbs*
One-of-a-kind amber massages, the oriental art of relaxation, chocolate peelings: recharge your batteries in style between the handmade furniture from Bali in the *Farmona Wellness & Spa* → **p. 71**

● *In the villa's garden*
In the 16th century, the *Decius Villa* was outside the city. Even today, its park with the charming café and sculptures by the artist Bronisław Chromy remains an oasis of tranquillity → **p. 49**

● *Intoxicating views at dinner*
An evening meal in the time-honoured *Wentzl Restaurant* is a feast for the senses in itself. But with the view of the Rynek Główny and illuminated St Mary's Church the pleasure is absolutely perfect → **p. 58**

● *Do not forget your swimming gear*
Why not combine a city and beach holiday? The artificial *Kryspinów Lake* just outside Krakow offers all kinds of summer relaxation → **p. 71**

● *Chill out in ideal surroundings*
The name of the *Chill Out Club* says it all: How about smoking a hookah while listening to relaxing music? Or what about a drink on a bench in the garden on a balmy summer evening? And the great snacks? They make a lazy afternoon even more enjoyable → **p. 72**

● *Swaying gently*
The city drifts slowly past you while a gentle breeze wafts over the railing: a *boat trip on the Vistula* offers an ideal alternative to the usual city sightseeing tour → **p. 99**

INTRODUCTION

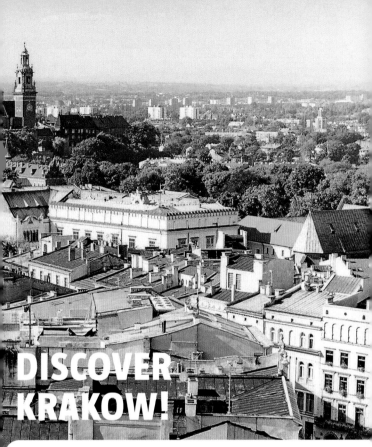

DISCOVER KRAKOW!

Krakow has a rich and eventful history, but visitors to the city will find no trace of the stuffy atmosphere experienced in some museums. The metropolis on the Vistula River is full of energy and exudes an almost southern joie-de-vivre. The city appears to be charmed in more than one respect. It was protected from destruction for centuries and became one of the most important centres of scholarship in Europe in the 14th and 15th centuries, providing a place for artists, freethinkers, philosophers and intellectuals to develop their ideas without interference from religious or political authorities.

This has all helped make the gem on the Vistula the most visited city in Poland. Krakow's unique atmosphere, a mix of culture and vitality, of history and modernity, of the future and legends, attracts guests from all over the world. More and more come every year – to walk in Copernicus's footsteps, to take part in festivals and make a journey though time in the midst of immortal architecture – or simply to enjoy life in the restaurants, cafés and clubs that are on a par with those in larger metropolises.

Photo: View of the castle and cathedral from St Mary's Church

Krakow has a big heart; in fact it is one of the world's largest: the Rynek Główny, the main square in the centre of the Old Town measures 200 × 200m – a space whose width alone makes a great impression in the middle of the sea of houses arranged like a chessboard around it. Krakow's heart is surrounded by absolute beauty, by houses and other buildings of every conceivable architectural style and period. The metropolis on the Vistula has managed to survive the last 800 years more or less unscathed and has protected its treasures and heritage to this day. It is also anything but a museum: city life centres around this square, this is where the people from Krakow meet, this is where the action is – and that until late at night and deep under the ground.

> **Krakow really starts to buzz on summer evenings**

Many of the more than 100 cafés, restaurants, bars and clubs around Rynek Główny that get Krakow's nightlife into full swing – especially on warm summer evenings – are located in traditional brick vaults below street level. The city's lifelines go deep. In the 13th century, the Vistula had frequently caused flooding, so it was simply decided at the time to raise the entire centre to a higher level. When living space became scarce 600 years later, people remembered the underground streets, excavated the endless corridors and used them as storehouses and hiding places, or just for enjoyment – and that is something night owls still do today. The people from Krakows like to go out and have a good time; the watering holes are full day and night. There is a common saying that 'People work in Warsaw but live in Krakow.'

Krakow had a hard time getting over the fact that the royal court moved to its unloved sister, which then became the capital, 400 years ago. However, the city compen-

Reminiscent of Vienna and the fin-de-siècle: fiacres on the Rynek Główny

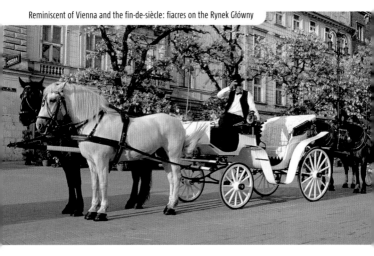

sated for its fall into relative unimportance in its own way: it became a magical city, the protector of stories and legends, the patron of poets, musicians and painters.

The fact that Krakow is considered to be Poland's cultural capital is not only due to the splendour of its architectural monuments, which led to the entire centre being named a Unesco World Heritage Site. Its reputation is further supported

> **Poland's cultural capital and its treasures**

by the large number of theatres, concert halls, galleries and museums to be found in what – with a population of 750,000 – is a relatively small city. In addition, there is a jazz scene that connoisseurs think can only be compared with New York and many world-famous artists, including the film director and Oscar prizewinner Andrzej Wajda and the composer Krzysztof Penderecki, one of the leading Polish avant-garde musicians, live and work in Krakow. The Nobel Prize laureate for literature Wisława Szymborska spent most of her life in the city on the Vistula and died there in February 2012. We should not forget klezmer music, the traditional Jewish folk music either, which is as vital as ever and underlines Krakow's importance as a former centre of Jewish life in Europe.

Krakow's Jewish heritage is concentrated in Kazimierz; the formerly independent town was incorporated around 1800. Expelled from Krakow in 1495 by the then king, following a series of pogroms, many Jews settled in Kazimierz and it developed into an important centre of their culture. The peaceful coexistence with the Catholic neighbours lasted until the German occupation of Poland in 1939. Only around 4000 of the 60,000 Jews living in Kazimierz survived the Nazi horror. Director Steven Spielberg paid tribute to the suffering of Krakow's Jews – in 1939, they were 25 percent of the population – and the industrialist Oskar Schindler, who saved more than 1100 forced

labourers from being murdered, in his film 'Schindler's List'. Today, Kazimierz has managed to preserve its unique flair; one in which the happy times of the past have come to life again: at the end of June and early in July, the Festival of Jewish Culture, probably Krakow's most important festival, is held in Kazimierz. It is a youthful, hip district, popular with students and artists, an in-place for night owls and party-goers, who have fun all night in summer and hunt for retro chic at the flea markets.

Centuries-old Krakow emanates a feeling of youthful freshness. The more than 120,000 students make it a young city and its dynamic development can also be seen in the establishment of state and private universities. They have taken their place alongside the oldest university in Poland and one of the oldest in the world: it was founded in 1364. Wawel Hill, with the Wawel Royal Castle and Wawel Cathedral – tourist highlights – was settled more than 50,000 years ago. There is proof that salt mining was carried out near Krakow starting around 1400 BC.

> **Teach and learn: Krakow has been a university town since 1364**

Krakow was first mentioned in a document in 965, indicating that the settlement on Wawel Hill had developed into an important trading centre along the salt and amber route. Krakow grew, became an episcopal see and capital city and also had to

View of St Mary's Church from the Rynek Główny

survive devastating strikes by the Tatars in the 13th century. The trumpet call that can be heard every hour from the tower of St Mary's Church recalls these attacks: the *hejnal* then stops abruptly, a reminder that the lookout was hit by an arrow while he was blowing his warning – another example of how far back Krakow's history reaches and how it still has its place in present-day life. This trumpet call is also transmitted live throughout Poland on the radio at midday. Krakow experienced its heyday in the 15th and 16th centuries, which is clearly visible in the magnificent Renaissance architecture. The city attracted artists, progressive thinkers and scholars. Nicolaus

Copernicus, who would later create a new view of the universe, was just one of the many who studied at Krakow University. There are more than 400 sights within the Planty, a green belt encircling the old city. These include town houses, palaces, famous museums with collections of international and Polish art and, last but not least, 60 churches. The number of houses of worship funded by queens, the nobility and rich citizens provides striking evidence of the city's wealth. The world-famous treasures in the churches, such as the altar created by the sculptor Veit Stoß in St Mary's Church, attract art lovers and pilgrims alike.

Krakow has always been a centre of religious life in Poland and played a significant role as a diocese and site of the coronation of the country's kings. It is often called a 'Papal city', although Karol Wojtyła, the later Pope John Paul II, was not born here but in Wadowice. However, Wojtyła spent more than 40 years in Krakow and left an indelible mark on the city. The man who was to become Archbishop of Krakow opposed those in power during the Nazi occupation by studying theology although it was forbidden. He later celebrated open-air masses in any weather to protest against the anticlerical Socialist regime, which in post-war Poland banned the workers in Nowa Huta from building a church. His, and the workers' opposition finally bore fruit: one year before being elected Pope, Karol Wojtyła consecrated the 'Ark of the Lord' Church in Nowa Huta. Krakow and Socialism is an interesting consideration

Centre of religious life in Poland

in itself. It is hard to imagine two more opposing mindsets: on the one hand, the city of liberals, of freethinkers and dissenters and, on the other, the regime who saw no place for these bourgeois tendencies in their classless society. That is why those in power quickly had the district of Nowa Huta and its steelworks built, their idea being to take the wind out of the sails of bourgeois resistance through the creation of a settlement for proletarian workers. However, the result was completely the opposite; it was precisely these workers and their strong adherence to the Catholic church that finally brought about the collapse of the system.

The steelworks are now history; people have come to terms with the upheaval caused by the end of Socialism and the opening of the country in the 1990s. Today, Krakow's main income comes from tourism and its role as an administrative centre. The city is the main provider of work in the region; the unemployment rate is 7%, significantly lower than Poland's 12%. An increasing number of visitors pay their respects to Leonardo da Vinci's 'Lady with the Ermine', admire the Cloth Hall in the Market Square and stroll through Nowa Huta. Krakow's inhabitants are fully aware that they live in a very special city – and they are proud of it. They love and cultivate its history and traditions and know how to celebrate for days on end – no matter whether the festivities are religious or of a more worldly nature. It is also said that the locals are thrifty if not downright stingy. That might be true, but they are also hospitable and cosmopolitan. That is why some people, including the violinist Nigel Kennedy, fall so deeply in love with the city that they choose to stay, live and work there – and thus play a role in the further chapters of Krakow's eternal history.

WHAT'S HOT

1

In the milk bar

Down-to-earth Krakow was the birthplace of the *Bar Mleczny* ('milk bar') – a Polish form of cafeteria – and this is also where its revival began. The simple restaurants are increasing in popularity all over Poland and more and more trendy young people have discovered their charm. The *U Pani Stasi (ul. Mikolajska 16)* is one of those in vogue at the moment and you might find it hard to get a place at lunchtime. The *Bar Dworzanin (ul. Foriańska 19)* has a salad bar in addition to *pierogi* and co. If you want to learn more about typical home-style cooking, take a culinary stroll through *www.about-poland.com/polish-food.html*

Very attractive

2

Fashion Krakow's designers like it a bit off-beat. *Studio B3 (at Flower & Banana, ul. Józefa 11)* pays particular attention to the details of their creations: gathers, pleats, appliqués. *Fama (www.fama.krakow.pl)* focuses on cool cuts and silhouettes while *Atelier Femini (ul. św. Jana 5, photo)* has made a name for its cheerful creations.

Coffee with culture

3

Artistic delights As weary sightseers relax over a cup of coffee or tea, they will find their eyes drawn to the walls of the cafés. An increasing number of them are now displaying art. The temporary photo exhibitions in the *Mlynek Café (pl. Wolnica 7)* provoke a lot of lively discussions. *Café Pod Kasztanowecem* is another artistic hotspot. The café is part of the *Wyspiański Museum (ul. Szczepanska 11)*. Works of art not only have their place on walls but also on shelves. That is how they feel in *Massolit (ul. Felicjanek 4, photo)*. The colourfully decorated café has a large library of English language books.

Your very own loft

A nice place to lay your head An increasing number of visitors to Krakow stay in flats rather than in one of the hotels. In this case, we are not talking about normal holiday flats but urban lofts in the best districts in town. The studios in *La Gioia Apartments (www.lagoiaapartments. com)* are perfect for fans of modern design. Carefully styled bathrooms, suspended staircases and integrated brick walls are all part of the look. The icing on the cake is provided by the sauna, whirlpool and fitness studio on the ground floor. Most of the flats offered by *Crakow Loft Apartments (www.cracowlofts.com)* are in historical houses and have the charm of old buildings in a big town – without any lack of comfort. The accommodation in the *Sebastiana Apartments (www.oldtown apartment.com)* is also extremely stylish.

Nightlife

Let your hair down In the eternal competition between Warsaw and Krakow, the capital city often comes in second best as far as nightlife is concerned. The nights in the old parts of Krakow are longer and the partying much wilder. International DJs set the mood in the *RDZA (ul. Bracka 3–5),* and the *Prozak (pl. Dominkański 6)* is almost as legendary as its line-up. It is also worth dropping into the *Club Fusion (ul. Floriańska 15):* there are often flamboyant fashion shows and artistic performances. *Frantic (ul. Szewska 4)* is famous for its atmosphere. You will forget what time it is on the sofas in the corners of this old vaulted cellar. *Kitsch (ul. Wielpole 15)* is especially popular with the gay crowd.

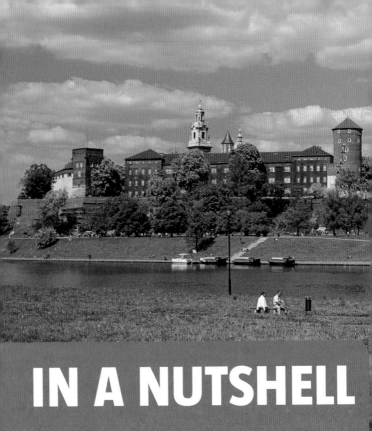

IN A NUTSHELL

FIN DE SIÈCLE

The connections between Vienna and Krakow became stronger during the Austrian annexation in the 19th century. During this period, the Polish city experienced cultural freedom to an extent it had not known since the Middle Ages — which is especially remarkable when compared with the areas occupied by Prussia and in Russian-ruled Warsaw at the time. There was a blossoming of theatre, satirical cabaret and literature; the city once again attracted painters, architects and writers. Especially in the second half of the 19th century, in the period art historians refer to as *Young Poland (Młoda Polska)*, the city was strongly influenced by the artists of the Viennese Secession and Paris.

The fin-de-siècle atmosphere found its expression in Art Nouveau: The young artists of the period wanted to follow new paths, deal with modern subjects, and work without any constraints. A group of painters, including Stanisław Wyspiański and Józef Mehoffer, the composer Karol Szymanowski and men of letters such as Tadeusz Boy-Żeleński formed a circle of intellectuals around Stanisław Przybyszewski and his wife Dagny Juel. Boy-Żeleński decried the miserliness of the conservative local population, their fear of new things

Photo: On the banks of the Vistula with a view of the Royal Castle and Wawel Cathedral

On art and legends, jazz and klezmer, kings and popes, princesses and dragons – and the magic of a city

and their narrow-mindedness. You can still see the paintings the artists paid their debts with in the *Jama Michalika Café (→ p. 54).* The largest collection of Polish art from the 19th century is on display in the Cloth Hall on the Market Square.

GALICIA

Galicia (officially: Kingdom of Galicia and Lodomeria, and the Grand Duchy of Krakow with the Duchies of Oświęcim and Zator) is the name given to those areas that now lie in Ukraine and Poland that were part of the Habsburg Monarchy between 1772 and 1918. The capital of Galicia was Lemberg (Lviv) – today, in the Ukraine – and Krakow became part of the kingdom in 1795 after the third partitioning of Poland. Although, as a result, the city on the Vistula experienced a very poor economic period,

Krakow has jazz in its veins; no day goes by without at least one exciting concert

in the cultural sphere, the province was given fairly free rein. Art and cabaret flourished as did Polish theatre and literature in Polish – in spite of the fact that the official language was German.

Today, cafés such as the *Noworolski* (→ *p. 55*) and *Kawiarnia Europejska,* and the *Hawełka* restaurant *(→ p. 57)* bring back memories of that period: the Hawełka even promotes itself as an 'Official Purveyor to the Imperial Court'. The fiacres on the Market Square remind one of Vienna, the city that acted as a model for Krakow in the fields of art and architecture during this period in history. And Austria's Emperor Franz Josef still looks down from the sign of the *Pod złotą Pipą Restaurant (Floriańska 30)* on the guests eating in the Gothic cellar. The name 'Galicia' experienced an inglorious revival in the years from 1941 to 1944: This is what the Nazis called the occupied 'General Government' area of Poland, of which Krakow was the capital.

JAZZ

Krakow is known as the capital city of Polish jazz, and one really does have the impression that you can hear this kind of music day and night coming out of the many cafés, restaurants and clubs. The phenomenon can be traced back to the early 1920s when the first real jazz bands started playing in Krakow. In Communist Poland after 1945, jazz was banned to the private sphere. Musicians performed in their flats; however, they did not only play music but also discussed politics and criticised the system. An underground scene gradually developed that only came to an end in 1954 when it was officially permitted to play jazz again. The first festivals were held in the 1960s: *Krakowska Jesien Jazzowa (Cracow Jazz Autumn)* is one of the most important jazz festivals in Europe and internationally renowned performers appear regularly on the city's stages.

The best place to listen to the quiet – and more classical – version of jazz is in *Piano Rouge (→ p. 71)* or *Stalowe Magnolie (→ p. 70)*. In contrast, *Indigo (→ p. 70)* and *Alchemia (→ p. 72)* invite artists who are more devoted to young, experimental jazz. This is where lovers of free, punk and avant-jazz will find what they are looking for and jazz that can even be danced to is served in the *Prozak (pl. Dominikański 6 | www. prozak.pl)* and *Ministerstwo (ul. Szpitalna 1 | www.klubministerstwo.pl)* clubs. The world-famous violinist Nigel Kennedy, who has lived there since his marriage, has become the best advertisement for the Krakow jazz scene. The man who studied under Yehudi Menuhin often joins Polish colleagues for spontaneous jam sessions in pubs like the *Piec Art (→ p. 71).*

KLEZMER

The first written reports on the *klezmorim,* travelling musicians who played traditional Jewish melodies, date from the 15th century. Originally, they performed cheerful dance music at celebrations such as weddings and harvest festivals, but the music as it is performed today has its roots in the tunes played at the weddings of the Ashkenazi Jews of Eastern Europe in the 19th century. However, the mixture of ceremonial melodies and folk tunes also displays elements of the traditional music of the Ukrainian, Russian, Bulgarian and Romany peoples. In earlier times, the repertoire was handed down from one generation to the next and this led to the development of entire dynasties of klezmer musicians – for example, Leopold Kozłowski, who was born in 1918, is the last representative of the Brandwein dynasty and the last klezmer musician in Galicia to have composed and played this traditional form of Jewish music before the Holocaust. Over the years, klezmer music has developed further and, in America in particular, it has pursued a completely different course. However, in Poland as well, many young bands such as *Kroke (www. kroke.krakow.pl)* and *Nazar* are following in the footsteps of their ancestors and play their music on the traditional klezmer instruments – clarinet, violin and drums. You can listen to them in the synagogues and restaurants, in the Galician Museum and during the Jewish Cultural Festival.

LEGENDS

You will come across the myths and legends connected with the city and its his-

KRAKOW'S ARTISTIC DUO

Two great artists left their mark on Krakow at completely different times; one in the 15th and the other in the 19th century. Veit Stoß came to Krakow from Nuremberg in 1477. It is not really known where the sculptor and painter learned his art nor which works he created before leaving Nuremberg. He became famous with his monumental main altar for St Mary's Church. The 13m (43ft)-high and 11m (36ft)-wide altar is considered one of the great masterpieces of Gothic carving. After 19 years in Krakow, he left the city as a highly respected citizen and returned to Nuremberg where he created many other masterpieces before his death in 1533.

The main artistic personality of the fin-de-siècle in the 19th century was Stanisław Wyspiański, a man who could turn his hand to many things, who studied in Paris and made a name for himself as a painter and writer. He also designed furniture and complete interiors, the sets for his plays, and glass windows including those in the Franciscan Church. Nature, simple peasant life and Polish history are the leitmotifs of his creative work.

tory wherever you go in Krakow. The most famous one is probably the story about the dragon that used to live in a cave in Wawel Hill and devour the town's virgins. A shoemaker eventually used a clever trick to get the better of the dragon: He threw a sheep stuffed with sulphur, pitch and pepper into the cave; the beast ate it and soon had a very upset stomach. In an attempt to quench his thirst, he drank so much water from the Vistula that he exploded. As a reward for his action, the shoemaker was offered the princess's hand in marriage!

The dragon does in fact live on: he strolls across the Rynek Główny, can be bought as a cuddly toy at any stand, and a parade of colourful dragons even makes its way through the city in summer.

Even the pigeons on the Market Square are part of a legend: they are supposedly knights whose lord had borrowed money from a witch and were then turned into birds because of their master's debts. That is why pigeons are not driven away from the square.

The trumpet signal that resounds from St Mary's Church every hour and can be heard throughout the country on the radio at midday recalls the attack by the Tatars in the 13th century. It is not the only reminder. The *lajkonik*, a man in a Tatar costume, also brings back memories of these violent times. In summer he walks over the marketplace and tries to touch everybody there with his sceptre. Let him – it is said to bring luck!

MOUNDS

There are four artificial hills in the city. Two are pre-Christian burial mounds (*Kopiec Wandy* in Nowa Huta and *Kopiec Krakuska* in Podgórze). The entire population of the city helped to pile up the soil for the third, the *Kościuszko Mound*, in 1820. It is named in honour of the leader of the

first uprising against the Russian occupiers in the year 1794. The fourth artificial hill, the *Piłsudski Mound*, was created in 1937 in remembrance of Marshal Józef Piłsudski the leader of the Polish legions in the First World War and contains soil from all of the battlefields Polish soldiers fought on. The latter two mounds are in the Las Wolski (Wolski Forest) and there is a lovely panoramic view from the ◆ Kościuszko Mound.

VISTULA

The Vistula (Wisła in Polish) is Poland's longest (1045km/650mi) river. It is still rather young when it flows through Krakow because its source is only 100km (62mi) to the south-west on Barania Góra. It makes its way through the entire country in two wide curves, crosses Warsaw and then flows into the Baltic not far from Gdańsk (Danzig). The river played a major role in the founding and development of Krakow; it was important both strategically and as a trade route. The Vistula was mainly used for transport as it was the only way salt, lead and wood could be delivered to the Baltic region in exchange for precious fabrics, amber and herrings. Today, the Vistula is one of Krakow's main tourist attractions. Although it is forbidden to go swimming in the river, it is popular as a place for water sports and boat excursions to the Benedictine abbey in Tyniec and other destinations. The Vistula also turns into a great place for partying in summer: The locals enjoy being near the river on the docked ships where they can eat, drink and dance; it is even possible to stay in one of the floating hotels. Most of the moorings are at the bottom of the Wawel Hill and On Bulwar Czerwieński in Kazimierz. On Bulwar Wołyński on the other bank, there is a sandy beach, a floating swimming pool and the *Hiflyer (9am–10pm | ticket 36 Pln | tel. 511 80 22 02 | www.hiflyer.pl)*, a firmly anchored balloon with a platform 200m (656ft) above the ground with a spectacular view over Krakow. Several festivals are also held along the Vistula and it is a popular place for families to enjoy a picnic. The loveliest area for walking or jogging is the section between the Wawel Hill and the bridge in Podgórze (Most Piłsudskiego). A new pedestrian bridge (kładka Bernatka), which is illuminated at night, connects Kazimierz with Podgórze.

KAROL WOJTYŁA

Karol Wojtyła, the later Pope John Paul II, moved to Krakow after graduating from high school and lived in the town on the Vistula until he was elected head of the Catholic Church in 1978. Wojtyła studied Polish philology at Krakow University and was one of the founders of the Teatr Rapsodyczny theatre group, in which he acted during the Nazi occupation. The Pope wrote poems and plays that are still performed in Poland's theatres today. During the German occupation in the Second World War, he studied theology in a forbidden 'underground seminary' and had to toil as a forced labourer in a chemicals factory and quarry.

Wojtyła was ordained as a priest in 1946 and served as vicar of St Florian's Church until 1951. He was elected bishop in 1958 and archbishop in 1963. He moved into the Bishop's Palace on ul. Franciszkańska where there is now a 'Pope's window' in honour of the speeches he held there. Together with the Solidarność trade union, he was a staunch opponent of the Socialist regime in Poland. It is therefore no surprise that there are always white and yellow flowers in front of the 'Pope's window' and that candles are always lit in memory of this Polish pope. He even has his own cake: the 'papal slice' *(kremówka papieska)* actually comes from Wadowice but it is also eaten in Krakow.

Memories of a defiant Krakow hero: bust of Pope John Paul II

THE PERFECT DAY
Krakow in 24 hours

08:00am THE DAY AWAKENS IN THE HEART OF THE CITY

Breakfast in the *Kawiarna Noworolski → p. 55* will prepare you for the day ahead and bring back memories of Krakow in the times of the Austro-Hungarian Empire. If you sit outside, you can enjoy the splendid view of the heart of the city – the *Cloth Hall → p. 34* the *Rynek Główny → p. 33*, *St Mary's Church → p. 31* – and will be able to see how the new day begins. Freshly fortified, you can hunt around the stands in the Cloth Hall in search of souvenirs such as beautiful amber rings.

10:00am TO THE UNIVERSITY WITH COPERNICUS

Walk past the *Town Hall Tower → p. 35* until you reach the university district. A visit to the museum of the *Collegium Maius → p. 30* will take you back in time to the Middle Ages and the days when Copernicus was studying in Krakow. His astronomical instruments are among the many exhibits on display. Don't miss out on the chimes of the *Glockenspiel → p. 30* in the university courtyard: it plays the melody of the popular students' song 'Gaudeamus Igitur' ('So Let Us Rejoice') at 11am sharp.

11:15am THE MASTER ALTAR

Now return to Rynek Główny, the Market Square. Stroll past St Adalbert's Church to St Mary's Church where the world-famous *Veit Stoß Altar → p. 31* is opened at 11.45am. A large crowd is always waiting to admire this masterpiece of carved wood and gold leaf – so make sure that you are there at least 15 minutes early!

12:00pm TRUMPETS & PAINTINGS

Now it is off to your next appointment; this time on St Mary's Square. The *trumpet call → p. 32* (photo left) from the tower of St Mary's Church is transmitted by radio all over Poland and recalls a Tatar attack in the 13th century. Afterwards, if you are ready for a break, the *Café Szal → p. 34* in the Cloth Hall offers a fabulous view of St Mary's Church. You can then decide if you want to go up or down: up to the *Polish Picture Gallery → p. 34* on the second floor of the Cloth Hall or down to the *Underground Museum → p. 34*, which has an exhibition on the history of the city.

01:15pm ON PALACES, THE CASTLE AND CATHEDRAL

Now walk along ul. Grodzka past the *Franciscan Church → p. 30* and Church of Saints Peter and Paul until you reach the oldest part of town and *ul. Kanonicza → p. 38* with

Get to know some of the most dazzling, exciting and relaxing facets of Krakow – all in a single day

bishops' palaces from all periods. The Wawel, the former seat of Poland's kings, rises up in front of you. After visiting *Wawel Cathedral → p. 38* and the *Royal Castle → p. 41* (photo right) you will be able to enjoy the view of the Vistula.

02:30pm JEWISH HISTORY

The next destination on your walking tour is Kazimierz where the *Synagoga Stara → p. 45* and *Old Jewish Cemetery → p. 44* (photo lower left) will tell you a great deal about the city's Jewish history. You will also be able to try Jewish specialities in one of the many restaurants, such as the *Klezmer Hois → p. 59*

03:45pm JOURNEY IN TIME TO THE KRAKOW GHETTO

You will be able to learn more about the tragic history of the Jewish ghetto and forced-labour camp in Płaszów in the museum housed in the *Pharmacy under the Eagle → p. 49*. A visit to the *Schindler Factory → p. 46* will provide you with more information about life in Krakow during the German occupation. In addition to photos and documents, there are several multimedia stations (also in English) and many stills from Steven Spielberg's film 'Schindler's List' are on display in the museum's café.

06:30pm EAT, HAVE FUN, LISTEN TO CLASSICAL MUSIC

Back in the old part of town, you can relax at a concert in St Adalbert Church or the *Church of Saints Peter and Paul → p. 37*. If you did not eat while you were in Kazimierz, then take a culinary break in the *Wesele → p. 58*. Still looking for some fun? Drop in at the cult pub *Alchemia → p. 72* on *Plac Nowy → p. 43*; there is a crocodile over the bar, no electricity and the floor is from an old church. Jazz aficionados will find what they love best in *Harris Piano Jazz Bar → p. 70* or at one of the many other venues near the main Market Square.

The Old Town, Kazimierz and Podgórze can be explored on foot.
Buy hourly or weekly tickets if you want to take a bus or tram.

SIGHTSEEING

CITY WHERE TO START?
The best place to start discovering Krakow is the **Rynek Główny (110 B–C3)** (*D 4–5*): Here you will find many of the main attractions and the best restaurants. The square is mainly reserved for pedestrians. You should park your car on a side street *(Parking tickets from machines: 3.10 Pln/hour, only cash)*, at the car park near the Franciscan Church *(pl. Wszystkich Świętych 5)* or the one at Westerplatte 18. All tram lines go to the centre of town.

Krakow, once the capital of the monarchy, charms its visitors with its medieval architecture and countless churches and museums.

The centre is not very large and is easy to explore on foot. The Wawel – home to the Royal Castle and the Cathedral – towers over the Old Town where you will find most of the main sights; many of them on the Royal Way. The Planty, a green belt of parks and avenues, was laid out where the city walls once stood and now forms a ring around the centre. The individual districts of Krakow, such as Kazimierz, Zwierzyniec and Kleparz, are grouped around this beautiful parkland.

Photo: Dome of the Teatr Słowackiego

The city of churches where you will feel the heartbeat of Poland's history: Krakow cultivates its centuries-long tradition

Most of them are also easy to walk to from the old part of town. You will only need a tram or bus if you want to visit one of the outer suburbs such as the workers' district Nowa Huta. Founded by the Russian occupiers, Nowa Huta was originally planned to be an ideal form of a Socialist city.

If you are of a romantic nature, try a horse-drawn carriage; it is like being trans-ported back to the days of the Austro-Hungarian Monarchy. Another alternative is to discover the city from the water from a passenger ship or boat on the Vistula. Later, when you want to relax after the hustle and bustle of the metropolis, take an excursion to the pleasant green resi-dential area of Wola Justowska or to Las Wolski (Wolski Forest), the largest forest park in Poland.

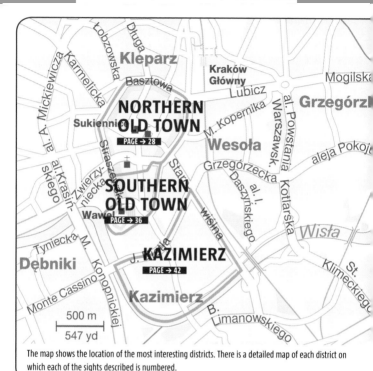

The map shows the location of the most interesting districts. There is a detailed map of each district on which each of the sights described is numbered.

NORTHERN OLD TOWN

Today's inner city consists of the Gothic Krakow of its founding years.

The settlement on the Vistula was granted its full rights and privileges as a town in 1257 and it was the capital city of the Polish monarchy until the end of the 16th century. It was only then that Warsaw took over the role. The golden age of the largest city in the country at the time lasted from the 13th to 15th century. The most beautiful churches, palaces and residences were created in this period and – unscathed by war – they now tell the story of Krakow's past. The first section of the Royal Way, with the most important and interesting buildings, runs through the northern part of town. The name recalls the old custom under which all the kings and important guests who made official visits to the city had to take this prescribed route to Wawel Castle. It starts at St Florian's Gate, continues along u. Floriańska to the centre, across the Rynek Główny and on to the Wawel, the hill with the Royal Castle and Wawel Cathedral. There is plenty of life in this part of Krakow; this is where people come for a stroll and where you will find many of the best restaurants and most expensive shops and boutiques.

1 FORTIFICATIONS ⚜

(110 C1–2) (*ﬄ E3–4*)

In the Middle Ages, Krakow was protected by a strengthened double wall, of up to 3m in width, and 47 towers. The individual guilds took care of these bastions and also sometimes stored their weapons there. The walls were surrounded by a moat and the city was made even safer in the 15th century with the addition of the *Barbakane* (barbican), a fortified outpost with seven slender turrets.

In the 19th century, most of the large European cities tore down their medieval defences, and it was also planned to dismantle all of Krakow's fortifications. However, a small section of the inner walls with two bastions and the arsenal, barbican and main portal have been preserved. It is only possible to inspect the fortifications from the outside, but you can go up to the top of the barbican and walls. There is a ⚜ nice view. A permanent exhibition gives information on the development and history of the complex and further details are provided in two or three temporary shows every year. Artists offer their pictures for sale inside the walls in summer and INSIDERTIP regular concerts and jousting festivals are also held here.

Leave the fortification complex through the main gate, the *Porta Gloriae,* to return to the city; this is where the Royal Way begins and it opens up a spectacular view of the ul. Floriańska with St Mary's Church and the Rynek Główny. *May–Oct daily 10.30am–5.30pm | entrance fee 6 Pln (barbican and walls) | entrance to the walls from ul. Pijarska*

MARCO POLO HIGHLIGHTS

2 COLLEGIUM MAIUS ★ ●
(110 A3) (*C5*)

The Jagiellonian university was the first academic institution of its kind in Poland and is also one of the oldest seats of learning in the world. It was founded by King Kasimir the Great in 1364. The oldest university building in Krakow, the Collegium Maius, with its Gothic inner courtyard, also

Gothic splendour in St Mary's Church

dates from this period. The eye-catching crystalline vaulting in the arcades around the courtyard is more reminiscent of a monastery than a university. If you do not happen to be here when the 'glockenspiel' is chiming – this happens every two hours, attracts many visitors, and ends with the song 'Gaudeamus Igitur' ('So Let Us Rejoice') – sit in the café in the original Gothic cellar and let yourself be transported back to the 15th century, to the time when Nicolaus Copernicus was studying here. There was a monument to the astronomer in the inner courtyard until the 1960s, and he is, along with Pope John Paul II, one of the university's most famous students.

You must also visit the University Museum: the 40-minute tour takes you through the magnificent Gothic rooms of the library, the professors' dining room and the main lecture hall. *Mon–Fri 10am–2.20pm, Sat 10am–1.20pm, April–Oct Tue/Thu to 6pm; Glockenspiel 9, 11am, 1, 3, 5pm (free) | entrance fee 12 Pln | ul. Jagiellońska 15*

3 KOŚCIÓŁ FRANCISZKANÓW (FRANCISCAN CHURCH) ★
(110 B4) (*D5–6*)

The Franciscan Church is the only religious building from the Art Nouveau period in Krakow. The exterior of the building is neo-Gothic but the interior is decorated with works by the Art Nouveau artist Stanisław Wyspiański. He painted the walls with flowers and stars and created the glass windows for the presbytery as well as the one above the main entrance with the 'Creation of the World'. The interior of the Franciscan Church is rather dark and you should INSIDER TIP choose a sunny day for your visit. The church also has interesting cloisters with portraits of the archbishops of Krakow including Karol Wojtyła. *Daily 6.30am–8pm, except during services | ul. Franciszkańska 2*

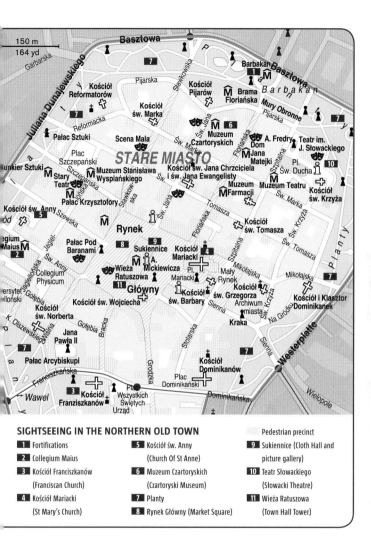

SIGHTSEEING IN THE NORTHERN OLD TOWN

4 KOŚCIÓŁ MARIACKI (ST MARY'S CHURCH) ★ (110 C3) (*m E5*)

Krakow's magnificent Gothic basilica dates from the 14th century but has been altered many times during its history. Both the exterior and interior of the house of worship thus display a mix of various ar-

chitectural styles. The greatest treasure in St Mary's Church is the *main altar created by the artist Veit Stoß*, who came to Krakow from Nuremberg and devoted twelve years of his life to this masterpiece. He started working on the 11 × 13m altar of oak and lime wood that he painted and decorated with gold leaf in 1477. The altar is opened at 11.45am from Monday to Saturday; it is an absolutely unique experience and attracts enormous crowds during the high season – so make sure to INSIDER TIP **arrive at least 15 minutes in advance!** Veit Stoß also created the figure of the crucified Christ in the southern side nave. It was carved out of a piece of sandstone and later inserted into the Baroque

5 INSIDER TIP KOŚCIÓŁ ŚW. ANNY (CHURCH OF ST ANNE)
(110 A3) (*∅ C4*)

The Baroque church was built by Tylman van Gameren in the early 18th century. The three-nave basilica is elaborately decorated and is the best example of late Baroque architecture in Krakow. The artist Baltasar Fontana decorated the church with stucco and illusionistic paintings, the

The heart of the museum of the same name: the collection of the aristocratic Czartoryski family

altar. You will have the most spectacular view over the city if you climb the more than 200 steps of the 54m (177ft)-high ✦ tower of the church. The best time to do this is on the hour when the *hejnał* resounds from the higher of the two towers; that is when men from the fire brigade plays 'Poland's second national anthem' live. *Church: Mon–Sat 11.30am–6pm, Sun 2–6pm; Tower: May–Sept Tue, Thu, Sat 9–11.30am and 1–5.30pm | entrance fee: church 6 Pln, tower 5 Pln | pl. Mariacki 1*

art form that attempts to create a sensation of three-dimensionality and depth in its works. The church is considered to be the most beautiful 18th-century building in Poland. *Only open during mass | ul. św. Anny 13*

6 MUZEUM CZARTORYSKICH (CZARTORYSKI MUSEUM) ★ ●
(110 C2) (*∅ E4*)

The oldest museum in the country has been undergoing renovations since the beginning of 2010, but it is hoped that the museum will open again in 2013. The museum was established on the estate of Princess Isabela Czartoryska – whose family not only loved wealth and luxury but also art – in Puławy in 1801. The collection mainly comprises works by European artists from the Middle Ages to the 19th century and includes Rembrandt's painting 'Landscape with the Good Samaritan'. Its greatest treasure however is 'The Lady with the Ermine' by Leonardo da Vinci. If you are lucky, you might be able to see the painting without crowds of other visitors – INSIDER TIP mornings during the week are a good time. The museum also has two other fine collections, one of arts and crafts through the ages and one on Polish history. The items of Turkish booty are particularly fascinating. They comprise the weapons and tents, that the Polish King Jan III Sobieski brought back to Krakow after winning a decisive battle in Vienna in 1583. *Tue–Sat 10am–6pm, Sun 10am–4pm | entrance fee 10 Pln | ul. Św. Jana 10 | www.muzeum.czartoryskich.pl/en*

▇ PLANTY

(110–111 A–D 1–5) (*ψ C–F 3–6*)
The 4km (2.5mi)-long green belt that encircles the Old Town was planted where the medieval city walls and moat used to be. When you take a stroll along the Planty with its shady avenues, ponds, flower beds and countless paths, you experience Krakow from another perspective – from the outside. An added attraction is the ● largest open-air collection of monuments that was created in the 19th and 20th centuries. The figures show great Polish artists, including the sculptor Wacław Szymanowski, as well as fictitious characters from Polish literature. The 50-acre green area in the centre of the city is a perfect training area INSIDER TIP for cyclists and joggers.

▇ RYNEK GŁÓWNY (MARKET SQUARE) ★ ●

(110 B–C3) (*ψ D4–5*)
Krakow's Market Square has always been – and still is – the centre of the city's cultural life. It is also the largest medieval square in Europe (200 × 200m) and is surrounded by the houses of Krakow's wealthiest citizens and the palaces of the aristocracy. The Sukiennice (Cloth Hall) and St Mary's Church are just two of the highlights of the Market Square. Until the 18th century, the square was jammed packed with small shops, the buildings of the Great and Small Scales, and the town hall, all of which were demolished after 1820. On a warm summer day, you will almost feel like you are in Italy; not only because of the many pigeons but also because of the Renaissance architecture of the Cloth Hall and residential buildings. The town houses on the square display diverse architectural styles – from Gothic to 20th century. Many of the facades are

extremely narrow; some only have two windows. There is a reason for this: the taxes the house owners had to pay was based on the number of windows overlooking the square. There are festivals, concerts and exhibitions throughout the year on the Rynek Główny, and it hosts Easter and Christmas markets.

9 SUKIENNICE (CLOTH HALL AND PICTURE GALLERY) ★
(110 B3) (*Ø D5*)

The Cloth Hall in the middle of the Market Square is one of the symbols of Krakow. This is where the most sought-after articles of the time – all kinds of cloth – and salt were traded: Krakow was on the old salt-trading route and enjoyed special privileges which made it the richest city in the Polish kingdom. The building itself was originally erected in the 14th century and altered in the 16th and 19th centuries. The long hall has external arcades and an original Renaissance parapet adorned with grotesque faces. The Cloth Hall still flourishes as a centre of commerce: there are shops selling amber jewellery, leather goods, products made of wood and other arts and crafts souvenirs on the ground floor.

The *Galeria Sztuki Polskiej XIX wieku (Gallery of Polish Painting and Sculpture from the 19th Century: Tue–Sat 10am–8pm, Sun 10am–6pm | entrance fee 12 Pln, audio guide 5 Pln | Rynek Główny 1–3)* has a collection of huge historical paintings and Polish portraits and landscapes on the first floor. The museum's ⚡ **INSIDER TIP** *Café Szał (daily 10am–11pm)* with a view of St Mary's Church is a joy for all the senses.

You walk through medieval Krakow beneath the market place when you visit the ● *Rynek Podziemny (Underground Museum: April–Oct Mon 10am–8pm, Tue 10am–4pm, Wed–Sun 10am–10pm, Nov–March Mon, Wed–Sun 10am–8pm, Tue 10am–4pm | entrance fee 17 Pln, free on Tue | Rynek Główny 1 | www.podziemiaryn ku.com).* The cemetery and miniature versions of small shops that used to be on the Market Square are especially fas-

Stylish trading place with a long history: the Cloth Hall on the Market Square

You almost wish the curtain would never go up: the magnificent Słowacki Theatre

cinating. You will also be able to see objects unearthed during excavations under the square. The most important aspects of Krakow's history are shown on screens (also in English).

⑩ TEATR SŁOWACKIEGO (SŁOWACKI THEATRE) (110 D2) (𝑚 E4)

The most beautiful theatre in Krakow was opened in 1893; it is an eclectic building decorated mainly with the neo-Baroque elements that were so popular in theatres under the Habsburg Monarchy at the time. This theatre was not only inspired by the architecture of Vienna but also that of the Paris Opera. Performances are in Polish but it still is worth visiting the theatre just to see the extravagant splendour of the interior. The INSIDER TIP original main curtain has been preserved and is one of the theatre's many highlights: it is not rolled up but raised and is decorated with an allegorical scene showing the personification of artistic inspiration, comedy and tragedy. It is only possible to visit

the theatre on an individually organised tour *(only available in Polish | tel. 01 24 24 45 25). Pl. Świętego Ducha 1 | www. slowacki.krakow.pl*

⑪ WIEŻA RATUSZOWA (TOWN HALL TOWER) ● ⤳ (110 B2) (𝑚 D5)

The town hall tower from the 14th century is 70m (230ft) high and stands in solitary splendour in the western section of the Market Square. Now there is a department of the Historical Museum of Krakow in the tower; it was originally part of the old town hall demolished in 1820. You can visit a room from the 14th century that was used as a treasury in the Middle Ages on the ground floor. The first floor houses the large hall that used to be used for the councillors' meetings. There is a INSIDER TIP splendid view over the city from the top floor and a café and small theatre in the town hall's cellar – the former prison and torture chamber. *May– Oct daily 10.30am–6pm | entrance fee 6 Pln | Rynek Główny 1*

SOUTHERN OLD TOWN

This section of Krakow is dominated by the silhouette of Wawel Royal Castle and Wawel Cathedral.

In the days of the Polish monarchy, Wawel Cathedral and the royal residence made Wawel Hill the most important area in Krakow. Before you make your way up the hill to immerse yourself in Polish history, you should take a closer look at the bishops' palaces on ul. Kanonicza. Take a break in one of the many cafés for an espresso and then admire the treasures in the Muzeum Erazma Ciołka.

Of course, you follow in the footsteps of former Pope John Paul II wherever you walk in Krakow, but you will feel that even more strongly here in this section of town. Karol Wojtyła lived on ul. Kanonicza while he was Bishop and then Archbishop of Krakow and worked in Wawel Cathedral, the church where bishops used to crown the Polish kings.

■ KOŚCIÓŁ ŚW. ANDRZEJA (ST ANDREW'S CHURCH)
(110 B–C5) (⌀ D–E6)

The church with the two characteristic towers is one of the oldest in Krakow and has managed to preserve its Romanesque appearance to the present day. Built in the 11th century and altered in the 13th and 14th, it is believed that it was the only house of worship to survive the attack by the Tatars in 1241 undamaged and to provide protection for the citizens. Baltasar Fontana adapted the interior of the small, three-nave church with the altar of black marble and pulpit in the shape of a ship to the Baroque style in the 17th century. It belongs to the neighbouring convent of the order of St Clare whose nuns lead a very strict life of secluded prayer and contemplation. *Daily 7am–6pm | ul. Grodzka 16*

KEEP FIT!

You can really work up a sweat in the *Pure Platinum Fitness Centre (Mon–Fri 6am–10pm, Sat/Sun 8am–8pm | ul. Podgórska 34, ground floor | tel. 01244 4111 | www.purepoland.com)* **(115 E2)** *(⌀ H7)* in the Galeria Kazimierz. In addition to fitness equipment, courses and a room for spinning, you will also enjoy the swimming pool, sauna, steam baths and solarium. After your (personal) training, cold drinks and coffee are served free of charge at the bar. The nicest tennis courts in Krakow are located in the parkland on the outskirts of the Wolski Forest in the *Wola Sport Paradise (ul. Koło Strzelnicy 5 | tel. 01 24 25 39 00 | www.wolasport paradise.pl)* **(117 D4)** *(⌀ 0)*. The indoor courts are open 24 hours a day, those outdoors from 6am to 10pm; it is also possible to hire tennis racquets. The best jogging track is near *Błonia* **(108 A6)** *(⌀ A5)*. A surfaced path runs around the meadow, some of it along the River Rudawa; it is also perfect for cyclists. Arguably the best *bike tour (cycle hire: see practical tips)* takes cyclists along the Vistula from Krakow to the Benedictine abbey in Tyniec. If you do not want to peddle back, you can take one of the ships that dock at the Wawel in Krakow.

The twelve Apostles welcome the faithful to the Church of Saints Peter and Paul

⬛2 KOŚCIÓŁ ŚW. PIOTRA I PAWŁA (CHURCH OF SAINTS PETER AND PAUL) (110 B–C5) (ⅉ D6)

The single-nave church built of red bricks and light-coloured granite, with individual chapels and a dome which can hardly be seen from outside, was the first Baroque church to be built in Poland. Construction started in 1597 and lasted until 1619 due to the problems with the statics of the dome. The house of worship is a typical example of the unadorned, early Roman Baroque style and is an exact copy of the Jesuits' church Il Gesù in Rome – some people go so far as to say that the proportions in Krakow are even better than those of the church it was modelled on. The interior was decorated with stucco by the Italian Giovanni Battista Falconi and there is a Foucault's pendulum in the dome to demonstrate the rotation of the earth. Concerts are often given in the church; posters at the entrance give full information on these events. However, it is always cold inside the building and you should not forget to have a pullover with you if you do decide to go to a concert. *Daily 6.30am–7pm, except during services | ul. Grodzka 54*

⬛3 MUZEUM ERAZMA CIOŁKA (ERAZM CIOŁEK MUSEUM) (110 B5) (ⅉ D6)

The museum is housed in the Gothic palace of Bishop Erazm Ciołek dating from the 16th century; it was totally renovated in the years between 1999 and 2006 and is now the home of one of the departments of the National Museum. The exhibition is divided into two sections: the most precious exhibits in the 'Art of Old Poland' collection are paintings and sculptures from the 14th to 16th century including a large number of Gothic altarpieces. INSIDER TIP The hall devoted to Baroque Polish funeral customs is particularly impressive; religious music plays in the background; on display are coffins and pictures of coffins that only exist in this form in Polish art.

'Orthodox Art of the Old Republic' shows icons – it is one of the oldest and most valuable collections of Orthodox painting in Central Europe – and objects used in the liturgy of the Eastern Church. *Tue–Sat 10am–6pm, Sun 10am– 4pm | entrance fee 12 Pln for each exhibition, free on Sun | ul. Kanonicza 17 | www.muzeum.krakow.pl*

4 ULICA KANONICZA (KANONICZA STREET) ★
(110 B5) (*ω D6*)

Every one of the houses in this narrow street is worth closer examination. The street is very busy during the day because this is the last section of the Royal Way (leading to the castle). That makes **INSIDER TIP** a stroll past the illuminated buildings on a warm summer evening particularly recommendable. The street is named after the people who lived on it: The canons of the cathedral chapter were the bishops' advisers and built their palaces here at the foot of the hill. The facades and richly decorated portals of the houses at number 1, 3, 9, 13 and 15 are especially interesting. Many of them have Renaissance arcaded courtyards behind their Gothic facades that are reminiscent of the Royal Castle on Wawel Hill – the bishops obviously wanted to keep pace with the king!

5 KATEDRA ŚW. STANISŁAWA I WACŁAWA (WAWEL CATHEDRAL)
● ☀ (110 B6) (*ω D7*)

Krakow's cathedral, next to the castle on the Wawel Hill, is the most important church in all of Poland – on account of its symbolism and function. The place in which Poland's kings used to be crowned is the third church on this site. Construction began in the 14th century and it was altered countless times over the centuries; it now combines all architectural styles from Gothic to modern. It is also the place where Poland's regents were buried and there are a large number of royal coffins

The street leads straight back to the Middle Ages: ulica Kanonicza

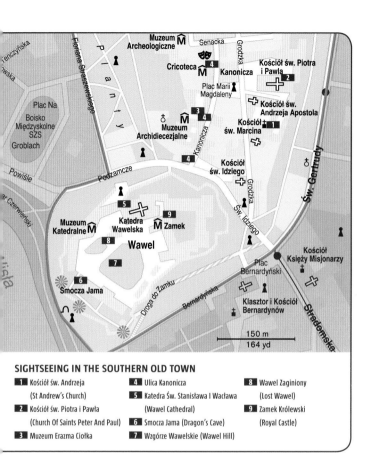

SIGHTSEEING IN THE SOUTHERN OLD TOWN

1 Kościół św. Andrzeja
(St Andrew's Church)

2 Kościół św. Piotra i Pawła
(Church Of Saints Peter And Paul)

3 Muzeum Erazma Ciołka

4 Ulica Kanonicza

5 Katedra Św. Stanisława I Wacława
(Wawel Cathedral)

6 Smocza Jama (Dragon's Cave)

7 Wzgórze Wawelskie (Wawel Hill)

8 Wawel Zaginiony
(Lost Wawel)

9 Zamek Królewski
(Royal Castle)

in the cathedral. President Lech Kaczyński and his wife, who both perished in a plane crash in April 2010, were also laid to rest in the crypt.

The three-nave basilica is flanked by two Gothic chapels – the one on the right, seen from the entrance, the *Holy Cross Chapel*, is especially noteworthy. It was decorated with Russian-Byzantine frescoes in the 15th century and is also the site of the marble grave Veit Stoß created for the Polish King Kazimierz Jegiellończyk. A Baroque silver sarcophagus with the

relics of St Stanisław occupies the central place in the cathedral.

The cathedral itself is rather small for a royal and episcopal church and that is why it is surrounded by chapels on all sides. Two are particularly precious: the *Kaplica Zygmuntowska (Sigismund Chapel)* and the *Kaplica Wazów (Waza Chapel)*. The first is described as the 'pearl of the Renaissance north of the Alps': the uniformity of its style and perfect symmetry is appreciated to this day, not only by art lovers. It was created out of red Hungarian marble, combined with white stone, by the Italian master Bartolomeo Berecci in the 16th century. The Waza Chapel represents the epitome of Baroque art and thought and is completely decorated with black marble. The skeletons on the bars of the door

Where Poland's kings were crowned and buried: Wawel Cathedral

are intended to remind visitors of the transience of life.

You should definitely visit the ✲ *Wieża Zygmuntowska (Sigismund Tower)* with the bell of the same name and enjoy the fabulous panoramic view. According to legend, all those who touch the bell are guaranteed eternal love and happiness in life. Objects from the treasury are displayed in the Cathedral Museum: chalices, monstrances, robes and exhibits with a connection to Pope John Paul II. *April–Sept Mon–Sat 9am–5pm, Sun 12.30–5pm, Oct–March Mon–Sat 9am–4pm, Sun 12.30–4pm | free admission to the Cathedral, Royal graves, Sigismund Tower and Museum 13 Pln, audio-guide 7 Pln | Wawel 1 | www.katedra-wawelska.pl/english*

6 SMOCZA JAMA (DRAGON'S CAVE)

(110 A6) (*🕮 C7*)

According to legend, the dragon that infamously devoured the town's virgins until it was outwitted by a clever trick used to live in this cave. There is probably a grain of truth to this ancient story: archaeologists found bones of prehistoric animals here. The tour of the illuminated Dragon's Cave starts at the top of Wawel Hill and ends down by the Vistula river. By the exit, there is an enormous metal figure of the dragon that belches fire every couple of minutes. *April–June and Sept/Oct daily 10am–5pm, July/Aug 10am–6pm | entrance fee 3 Pln | Wawel 5*

7 WZGÓRZE WAWELSKIE (WAWEL HILL) ✲

(110 A–B 5–6) (*🕮 D7*)

People were living on Wawel Hill long before Christianity reached the area around Krakow in the 10th century: archaeologists have discovered objects from the early

Stone Age here. The fact that the hill not only had wild springs but was also surrounded by the Vistula on all sides made it a strategically ideal location. Today, it is no longer possible to see where the Vistula originally flowed because the river was diverted in the 19th century. However, as you follow the Royal Way to the Wawel, you will pass the old river bed at the end of ul. Kanonicza. The hill is one of the best lookout points in the city.

8 WAWEL ZAGINIONY (LOST WAWEL) (110 B6) (𝑚 D7)

This archaeological and architectural museum shows reconstructions of Romanesque buildings that were found during excavations on the Royal Hill. Models and films are used to give an impression of the Wawel from the 10th to 14th century. The collection consists of stone relics, vessels, pieces of jewellery and other articles made of bone and wood that were unearthed here. The most interesting exhibit is the INSIDERTIP▶ almost completely preserved early-Romanesque rotunda from the 10/11th century dedicated to the Virgin Mary. *April–Oct Mo 9.30am–1pm, Tue–Fri 9.30am–5pm, Sat/Sun 11am–6pm, Nov–March Tue–Sat 9.30am–4pm, Sun 10am–4pm | entrance fee 8 Pln, April–Oct Mon, Nov–March Sun, free admission | Wawel 5*

9 ZAMEK KRÓLEWSKI (ROYAL CASTLE) ★ (110 B6) (𝑚 D7)

The castle was the first residence in the country to be built in the Renaissance style (1504–1536). King Zygmunt I Stary (Sigismund I of Poland) commissioned Italian artists from Florence to create the monumental three-storey building with its arcaded inner courtyard. It was the official residence of Poland's monarchs until the end of the 16th century. When part of the building was destroyed by fire,

it was reconstructed in the Baroque style but King Zygmunt III Waza and his court moved to Warsaw.

Today, there is a museum in the castle; all of the rooms – both the Private and Royal Chambers – are open to the public. The greatest treasure is the ● collection of tapestries from the 16th century that were commissioned by King Zygmunt August and woven out of silk in Brussels. They were made to measure for the rooms and originally covered most of the walls; they recount three of the most important stories from the Bible: Adam and Eve, the Tower of Babel, and Noah's Ark. *Reprezentacyjne komnaty królewskie (Representative Royal Chambers): April–Oct Tue–Fri 9.30am–5pm, Sat/Sun 11am–6pm, Nov–March Tue–Fri 9.30am–4pm, Sat/Sun 10am–4pm | entrance fee April–Oct 17 Pln, at other times 14 Pln, free on Sun; Prywatne komnaty królewskie (Private Royal Chambers): as above, closed Sun. | entrance fee 24 Pln, only with tour in Polish or English | Wawel 5*

The crown jewels are on the ground floor of the oldest section of the castle where you will also see the Gothic remains of the earlier building. The exhibits include silver platters and jugs and extravagantly decorated horses' harnesses. Pride of place is given to the *Szczerbiec*, the coronation sword of the Polish kings. Weapons from the 15th to 19th century, as well as medieval armour, are on display in the neighbouring armoury. *Skarbiec Koronny i Zbrojownia (Crown Treasury and Armoury): April–Oct Mon 9.30am–1pm, Tue–Fri 9.30am–5pm, Sat/Sun 11am–6pm, Nov–March Tue–Sat 9.30am–4pm | entrance fee April–Oct 18 Pln, Nov–March 16 Pln | Wawel 5*

You can buy tickets for the exhibitions at the entrance gate *(Brama Herbowa | only Fri–Sun)* or in the new *Information Centre (Centrum Promocji i Informacji)* where you will also find toilets, souvenir shops, a sub-post office, restaurants and cafés. There is a wonderful view from the terrace of the INSIDER TIP *Café Słodki Wawel* in summer. *April–June Mon–Fri 9am–4.45pm, Sat/Sun 10am–4.45pm, July/Aug Mon–Fri 9am–5.45pm, Sat/Sun 9.45am–5.45pm, Sept/Oct Mon–Fri 9am–4.45pm, Sat, Sun 9.30am–4.45pm, Nov–March Tue–Sat 9.15am–2.45pm, Sun 9.30am–2.45pm | Wawel 9 | www.wawel.krakow.pl, www.zamek-krolewski.pl*

Summer nights with a special flair: the fashionable fun spot Kazimierz

KAZIMIERZ

Kazimierz was an independent city until the 19th century. It is named after King Kazimierz Wielki who founded it in 1335. Over the years, Kazimierz developed into a large city with a marketplace, town hall and a number of magnificent monasteries. The Jews who were resettled there from Krakow in the 15th century had their homes in an enclosed section around ul. Szeroka. This Jewish world with its seven synagogues, cemeteries, businesses and schools functioned unchanged until the 19th century when the city council decided to tear down the walls and once again gave Jews the right to settle wherever they wanted. Their peaceful life ended in 1941: the National Socialist occupiers deported the Jewish population to the ghetto in the Podgórze district of Krakow. Kaziemierz's Jewish heritage is just one – albeit very important – part of its history: The Gothic Kościół Bożego Ciała (Corpus Christi Church) and Kościół Pauliów na Skałce (Pauline Church 'On the Rock') on the Vistula show that there are also interesting sights with a Christian background in Kazimierz. You should try to experience the special flair of Kazimierz in the evening, perhaps in one of the many Jewish restaurants on ul. Szeroka or at a concert of klezmer music. This is the trendiest district in Krakow: this is where partygoers, night owls and artists gather to enjoy themselves. Things become especially lively in summer when the cafés, pubs and clubs on Plac Nowy stay open until the early hours of the morning. *You can either walk to Kazimierz (15 min from the Wawel Hill via ul. Stradom and ul. Krakowska; from Poczta Główna via ul. Starowiślna) or by tram 3, 6, 8 (Wawel to Plac Wolnica) or 13 (Poczta Główna to Miodowa).*

1 KOŚCIÓŁ BOŻEGO CIAŁA (CORPUS CHRISTI CHURCH) ⭐
(114 B4) *(ⓜ F8)*

The parish church in Kazimierz on the former marketplace is one of the most beautiful Gothic churches in the city. According to legend, when the church was built a strange light could be seen for weeks above the construction site, a former swamp. When workers dug there, they discovered a monstrance that had disappeared from a church in Krakow. The medieval church was adapted to the Baroque style in the 18th century. The main altar and pulpit shaped like a boat are particularly lovely. *Daily 6am–8pm, except during services | ul. Bożego Ciała 26*

2 KOŚCIÓŁ PAULIÓW NA SKAŁCE (PAULINE CHURCH 'ON THE ROCK')
(113 E5) *(ⓜ D9)*

The Baroque church was built by Anton Müntzer and Antonio Solari on the site of a small Gothic predecessor in the 18th century. They created a three-nave basilica with two towers that worshippers entered through a magnificent portal of black marble. There is a legend that connects this site with the death of St Stanisław, the most important patron saint of the country. It is said that he was beheaded

where the church stands and his body then thrown into the nearby well. People claim that the water then took on healing powers and the well became a place of pilgrimage for believers from all over Poland. A solemn procession in honour of St Stanisław is organised every year on the Sunday after 8 May – it begins at the Wawel Cathedral and ends at the Pauline Church. *Daily 6am–8pm, except during service | ul. Skałeczna 15*

3 INSIDER TIP ▶ ŻYDOWSKIE MUZEUM GALICJA (GALICIA JEWISH MUSEUM)
(114 C3–4) *(ⓜ G8)*

This private museum is devoted to the memory of the victims of the Holocaust. The history of Jewish life in Galicia is exceptionally well documented in the exhibition 'Traces of Memory' by the photographer Chris Schwarz. His pictures take visitors on a journey through the eastern regions of today's Poland and the Ukraine. There is also a well-stocked bookshop with literature on Galicia and Jewish history, as well as a café, at the museum. *Daily 10am–6pm | entrance fee 15 Pln | ul. Dajwór 18 | www.galiciajewishmuseum.org*

4 PLAC NOWY (NEW SQUARE)
(114 B3) *(ⓜ F8)*

The square is still a lively marketplace, but the type of goods sold there has changed considerably. The Okrąglak hall in the middle was a kosher poultry abattoir until 1939. The meat that was slaughtered according to the rules of Jewish law was then sold at the market. You can buy delicious INSIDER TIP *zapiekanka* at the small snack bars in the Okrąglak. The cult snack for 5 to 7 Pln is a kind of Polish pizza; if you want to try it at the most popular stand *U Endziora*, you will probably have to queue up for a while. There is a food and flower market on the Plac Nowy every day and INSIDER TIP ▶ a flea market at the weekend where you will mainly find clothing, bags and jewellery (including designer articles at excellent prices). On Saturday, there are also antiques including many pieces of old Jewish silver. There are countless restaurants and fashionable pubs such as the *Alchemia* around the square that serve at outside tables in summer.

■5 SYNAGOGA REMUH (REMUH SYNAGOGUE) ★
(114 C3) (*Ø F7*)

The seven synagogues in Kazimierz have all been preserved and regular services are still held in the 16th-century Remuh Synagogue on the Sabbath (after sunset on Friday and on Saturday) and other Jewish holidays. The interior is very simple and unadorned in keeping with the commandment in the Old Testament of not using decorations from the living world in art. The orthodox division into separate sections for men and women is still discernible in the synagogue's architecture.

The neighbouring *Old Jewish Cemetery (Stary Cmentarz)* is no longer in use – burials now take place at the New Cemetery – but is well worth visiting to see its many old gravestones. The largest tomb is that of Iserles Remuh, a rabbi of the community in the 16th century, for whom Jews have the greatest respect and regard as a kind of saint. Today, Jews from all over the world still make pilgrimages to his grave as they believe that any prayers said there will be heard.

You will see remnants of *macevas* (Jewish gravestones) that were found during renovation work in the 1950s on the eastern wall to the right of the entrance to the cemetery. The locals call it the 'Wailing Wall' after the counterpart in Jerusalem. Men have to cover their head if they want to visit the synagogue or cemetery – if you do not have a cap with you, you can borrow a *kippah* free of charge in the synagogue. *Mon–Thu 9am–4pm (to 6pm in summer), Fri 9am–3.30pm (to*

The Remuh Synagogue is the only one in Krakow where services are still held

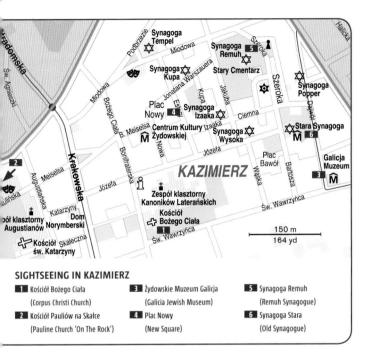

SIGHTSEEING IN KAZIMIERZ

1 Kościół Bożego Ciała
(Corpus Christi Church)

2 Kościół Pauliów na Skałce
(Pauline Church 'On The Rock')

3 Żydowskie Muzeum Galicja
(Galicia Jewish Museum)

4 Plac Nowy
(New Square)

5 Synagoga Remuh
(Remuh Synagogue)

6 Synagoga Stara
(Old Synagogue)

5.30pm in summer) | entrance fee 5 Pln |
ul. Szeroka 40

6 SYNAGOGA STARA
(OLD SYNAGOGUE)
(114 C3) (*∅ F8*)

Today, this Gothic synagogue, which was converted during the Renaissance, houses a Jewish museum. The temple dates from the end of the 15th century and is the oldest synagogue in Poland. You will notice the traditional separation into different sections for men and women even before you enter. The museum tells the story of everyday Jewish life: knives used for slaughtering animals following Jewish laws, circumcision instruments, crowns and bells for the Torah. *Mon 10am–2pm, Tue–Sun 9am–5pm | entrance fee 8 Pln,* ● *free admission Mon | ul. Szeroka 24*

IN OTHER DISTRICTS

DOM MEHOFFERA
(JÓZEF MEHOFFER HOUSE)
(108 C4) (*∅ B4*)

This museum is devoted to the work of one of Poland's greatest Art Nouveau painters: Józef Mehoffer (1869–1946) bought the house where Stanisław Wyspiański was born, a neo-Classicist villa in Nowy Świat, in 1932 and lived here with his family until his death. The house with the original furnishings, family photos and souvenirs of the artist is just as fascinating as his paintings and projects, such as the glass windows he designed for the Freiburg Cathedral. The **INSIDER TIP** garden next to the house, where Mehoffer created many of his pictures, is an oasis of greenery and the ideal place to take a break from sightseeing. *Wed–Sat noon–6pm, Sun 10am–4pm, garden and the museum's Café Ważka 10am–9.30pm | entrance fee 6 Pln, free admission Sun | ul. Krupnicza 26 | muzeum.krakow.pl*

FABRYKA SCHINDLERA (SCHINDLER FACTORY) ★ ●
(115 F5) (*ℳ J9*)

The Museum of the City of Krakow established the very powerful permanent exhibition on the fate of its Jewish and non-Jewish citizens 'Krakow under Nazi Occupation 1939–1945' on the premises of Oskar Schindler's Deutsche Emailwaren Fabrik (German Enamelware Factory) (D.E.F.). On the three floors of the museum, visitors can get a taste of what life was like for the people living in Krakow, learn about the horrible conditions in the ghetto and the long-awaited liberation by the Red Army in January 1945. The offices have been preserved in their original state in memory of Oskar Schindler who produced equipment for the German Army in his factory. Although Schindler was originally only interested in making money, he decided to save more than 1100 Jews from being sent to concentration camps after the Nazis liquidated the ghetto in March 1943; he pretended they were needed to produce materials essential to the war effort. Schindler's action became world-famous with Steven Spielberg's film 'Schindler's List' in 1993. *April–Oct Tue–Sun 10am–8pm, Mon 10am–4pm, Nov–March Tue–Sun 10am–6pm, Mon 10am–2pm | entrance fee 15 Pln, free on Mon | ul. Lipowa 4 | mhk.pl*

KOŚCIÓŁ JEZUITÓW (JESUIT CHURCH)
(111 E3) (*ℳ F5*)

This monumental three-nave, red-brick basilica with its 70m (230ft)-high tower

Inspiration for Art Nouveau artists: the small, but exquisite, garden of the Mehoffer House

was built in the Wesoła suburb between 1909 and 1921. The specific architectural details and the sculptures on the facade were carved out of light-coloured stone or cast in metal. In this building, the architecture Franciszek Mącyński successfully combined modern and traditional techniques: the vaults are made of concrete and iron while the mosaics are reminiscent of those in early Christian churches. The interior is especially interesting: The arches are decorated with paintings and golden mosaics. *Only during services | ul. Kopernika 26*

MOGIŁA (117 E4) (*ᗰ 0*)

In the Middle Ages, Mogiła was an independent village, located on the outskirts of Krakow, but today it is part of the Nowa Huta district. It was founded around a monastery: Cistercian monks started construction of the monastery and church around 1222. The final result was a three-nave basilica with two chapels on either side of the altar that was renovated in the 14th century and adapted to the Baroque taste of the time in the 17th century. The monastery itself is on the south side of the church and since Cistercian monks still live there, it is not possible to visit it. In spite of changes over the years, the church and monastery have preserved their medieval character. The Gothic Cross and paintings in the church, created by Stanisław Samostrzelnik in the 16th century, are of special interest. *Daily 7am–7pm, except during services | ul. Klasztorna 11*

Opposite the abbey, on the other side of the street, is Poland's oldest wooden church. The three-nave hall church *Kościół św. Bartłomieja (St Bartholomew's Church)* was built by the Cistercians for the people living in the village. The 15th-century Gothic building was made Baroque in the 17th century and decorated with illusionistic paintings. *Daily 7am–7pm, except*

during services | ul. Klasztorna 12 | tram 15: Klasztorna*

MOCAK (MUSEUM OF MODERN ART) (115 F5) (*ᗰ J9*)

The Museum of Modern Art, MOCAK for short, was opened in 2011 and presents exhibitions and projects reflecting the latest trends in Polish and international art on a surface area of 108,000ft². The permanent exhibition is complemented by interesting temporary shows. Parts of the Schindler Factory were used for the museum building together with completely new exhibition rooms. *Tue–Sun 11am–7pm | entrance fee 10 Pln, ● free on Tue | ul. Lipowa 4 | www.mocak.com.pl*

MUZEUM NARODOWE (NATIONAL MUSEUM) (108 B5) (*ᗰ A5*)

The holdings of the museum, which was founded in 1879, grew so quickly that it became necessary to move some of its departments to other locations, for example to the gallery in the Cloth Hall and the Czartoryski Museum. The most interesting sections in the main building are the military exhibition and a collection of Polish arts and crafts and especially the 'Gallery of Polish Art of the 20th Century'. The museum also houses *Tribeca Coffee (Mon 10am–3pm, Tue–Sat 10am–6pm, Sun 10am–4pm)*. *Tue–Sat 10am–6pm, Sun 10am–4pm | entrance fee 10 Pln, permanent exhibition free on Sun | Al. 3. Maja 1 | www.muzeum.krakow.pl*

NOWA HUTA (NEW WORKS) (117 E4) (*ᗰ 0*)

Nowa Huta was founded as an independent city near Krakow in 1949. It was intended to fulfil both an economic and political role: After the Second World War, the Russian occupiers decided to create a model Communist city where the inhab-

The huge sculpture of Jesus in the Ark of the Lord Church is very impressive

itants – who had been transported to Nowa Huta in vast numbers – would live their lives in modern concrete blocks of flats. Equally, Nowa Huta was intended to act as a counterpart to the bourgeois, intellectual centre Krakow as an independent workers' town with a perfect infrastructure and integrated workplace. The Lenin Steelworks was built at the same time as the first houses.

Nowa Huta also became famous for the *Ark of the Lord (daily 6.30am–6pm, except during services | ul. Obrońców Krzyża 1 | bus 139: Arka)*, the first church in the Socialist model community. The people living in Nowa Huta fought for more than ten years to get permission to build the church and many paid with their lives in the conflicts that took place. After an additional ten years of construction, the Ark of the Lord was finally consecrated by the then Archbishop Karol Wojtyła in 1977. Its modern architecture reminds one of

Le Corbusier's famous chapel in Ronchamp. The building in Nowa Huta is shaped like a large boat with the Cross as its mast. It was mainly constructed of round, light-coloured stones that the faithful had collected from rivers. The most impressive features of the interior are the wooden roof construction and enormous bronze sculpture of the crucified Christ. The tabernacle contains a crystal the crew of 'Apollo 11' brought back from the moon.

Until today, it has not been possible to merge Nowa Huta and the 250,000 people living there with the other districts of Krakow – the differences in culture and social structure are simply too great. In addition, the workers' district is now struggling with unemployment. After the steelworks were privatised, many of the workers were made redundant.

The most interesting architecture in Nowa Huta comes from the 1950s and 1960s and can be seen on *pl. Centralny (Central*

Square) the starting point for the four main roads and a pedestrian avenue *(Aleja Róż)*. These houses have a neo-Classicist character, the flats are large and sunny, and there are spacious parks nearby. The architecture from the later phase (1970s and 1980s) is completely different. Built quickly and cheaply, high, grey blocks of flats – with a planned 86ft² per person – set the tone in this section of town. Nowa Huta is fairly spread out; you should plan at least half a day for your visit. *Tram 1 (Teatr Ludowy), 4 (Plac Centralny), 15 (Cystesów), bus 139: Arka*

OGRÓD BOTANICZNY (BOTANICAL GARDENS) ●
(117 E4) (*Ш H–J 4–5*)

The most beautiful seasons in the Botanical Gardens are INSIDER TIP▶ summer and early autumn when the lilies, peonies and irises are in full bloom. The park with its strangely mysterious atmosphere was created from a section of the castle garden in 1783 and covers an area of almost 25 acres. The aristocratic Czartoryski family was behind the establishment of the gardens; the property was transferred to the Jesuits who subsequently sold it to Krakow University. An astronomical observatory was installed in the small Classicist castle at the end of the 18th century just as the first greenhouses were being erected.

The *Botanical Museum* is now housed in the former observatory. In addition to the largest collection of orchids in Poland, plant lovers will be charmed by the alpine flora, the water lilies blooming on the surface of the two ponds and a splendid collection of azaleas and rhododendrons. The oldest tree in the garden is a 500-year-old oak. You can easily walk to the green oasis from the Market Square via ul. Kopernika. *April–Oct daily 9am–7pm, palm houses Sat–Thu 10am–6pm | entrance fee 6 Pln | ul. Kopernika 27*

PODGÓRZE
(117 E4) (*Ш E–J 9–10*)

The Nazis set up the Jewish ghetto in a 49-acre section of today's suburb of Podgórze in March 1941. 16,000 people were forced to live where only 3000 had had their homes before – in unbelievably cramped conditions. Today, there is no wall or any special plaque to show where the ghetto was. Instead, an installation of metal chairs on *Plac Bohaterów Getta (Ghetto Heroes Square)* recalls the destruction of the ghetto in March 1943 when all of the furniture and personal belongings of the people living there were simply thrown out of the windows. The inhabitants were then either shot in the ghetto or transported to concentration camps such as Płaszów and Auschwitz. There is now a museum in the *Apteka Pod Orłem (Pharmacy under the Eagle);* the chemist's shop run by Tadeusz Pankiewicz was the only one that provided Jews with medicine and he saved many – especially children – by hiding them in the cupboards in his shop. The exhibition in the museum deals with the history of the ghetto and Płaszów concentration camp. *(April–Oct Mon 10am–2pm, Tue–Sun 9.30am–5pm, Nov–March Mon 10am–2pm, Tue–Thu/Sat 9am–4pm, Fri 10am–5pm | entrance fee 6 Pln, free on Mon | pl. Bohaterów Getta 18 | mhk.pl)*

WOLA JUSTOWSKA
(117 D4) (*Ш 0*)

The most beautiful and exclusive district of the city, which became part of Krakow in the 20th century, is not only interesting on account of the extravagant architecture of the villas and detached houses there but also its location: It is bordered on one side by the Las Wolski (Wolski Forest) with the zoo and many footpaths and, on the other, by the Rudawa River. The ● *Willa Decjusza (Decius Villa)* provides

sculpture of the fire-belching dragon on the Vistula – is also in the park. You will be able to admire his open-air creations and then enjoy a tasty cappuccino in the small café *(gallery and café daily. 11am–7pm). Only accessible during functions | ul. 28 lipca 1943 17a | www.villa.org.pl | bus 152: Park Decjusza.*

FARTHER AFIELD

AUSCHWITZ-BIRKENAU ★

(116 C4) *(m 0)*

No other name brings back more memories of the unimaginably horrible deeds perpetrated by the Nazis than that of the Auschwitz-Birkenau concentration camp. More than 1.2 million people – mostly Jews – were murdered in the largest German extermination camp. Today, there is a memorial site and museum on the 470-acre area near Oświęcim (about 45km/28mi from Krakow). The organisation of what was originally a labour camp shows just how the occupiers went about their work with such perfidious technocratic coldness: The prisoners in Camp III (Monowitz) had to labour in the factories of the Buna Werke (IG Farben) while those in Auschwitz I were forced to build roads and houses. The largest section of the camp was where the living barracks, prison, death cells, administration and the home of the camp's commander Rudolf Höß and his family were located. You can still see the cynical sign 'Arbeit macht Frei' (Work brings Freedom) above the main gate to Auschwitz I.

The real horror took place in Auschwitz II (Birkenau): People were murdered in four large gas chambers and then incinerated in the crematoriums – the wooden housing barracks were only temporary. A visit

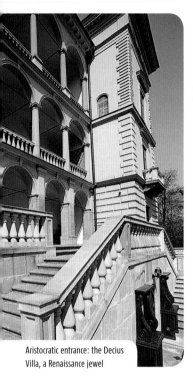

Aristocratic entrance: the Decius Villa, a Renaissance jewel

another good reason for visiting Wola Justowska. It was built in the 16th century by the former owner of the area, the royal secretary Just Decius. At the time, the Renaissance villa was a typical *villa suburbana,* located way out of town. During reconstruction work in the 17th century, it was given its present rectangular form and the large loggia. Although Krakow has grown around the villa over the centuries, it has managed to maintain its romantic character. The house is in a 25-acre park and also home to a luxury restaurant. In summer, the 'Forum for the Dialogue of Cultures' frequently organises concerts here.

The *gallery of the Krakow sculptor Bronisław Chromy* – one of his many works is the

to Auschwitz is a highly emotional – and shocking – experience; make sure that you, and especially your children, are well prepared for what you will encounter.

Auschwitz Camp: April–Oct only with guided tour (4 hours) | Tours in English April, Oct 12, May–Sept 10.30am, noon, 1.30pm | entrance fee 40 Pln, Nov–March free without tour; Museum: daily Dec/Jan 8am–3pm, March/Nov 8am–4pm, April/Oct 8am–5pm, May/Sept 8am–6pm, Jun–Aug 8am–7pm | entrance free | Więźniów Oświęcimia 20 | Oświęcim | www.auschwitz.org.pl | journey: mini-buses from Krakow Railway Station or by car via Dw 780, Dk 44 or A4 towards Oświecim; follow signpost 'Muzeum Auschwitz'

WIELICZKA

(117 E5) (*m 0*)

The salt mines in Wieliczka (10km/6mi to the south) are one of the main attractions in the environs of Krakow and have been a Unesco World Heritage Site since 1978. From the 13th century on, the mines were one of the most important sources of revenue for Krakow and the entire kingdom; in its heyday in the 15th century, the salt trade accounted for more than 30 percent of the town's total income. Mining continued until well into the 20th century but now very little salt is extracted.

There are more than 300km (186mi) of labyrinthine paths on nine underground levels. The main attraction – in addition to the 20m (66ft)-high chambers and a salt lake – is the Kaplica św. Kingi (Chapel of the Blessed Kinga) where everything down to the chandelier is made of pure salt. There is also a restaurant and souvenir shop beneath the ground. INSIDER TIP Don't forget your pullover: it is only 14°C (57°F)! *April–Oct daily 7.30am–7.30pm, Nov–March 8am–5pm, English tours 10, 11, 11.30am, 12.30, 1.45, 3, 5pm | entrance fee 64 Pln | Daniłowicza 10 | Wieliczka | www.kopalnia.pl | Journey: bus 304 (Filharmonia to Wieliczka kościół, bilet aglomeracyjny. 2.60 Pln) or by car over the A4 towards Tarnów to Wieliczka exit, signpost: Kopalnia (Mine).*

Salt as an artistic material: sculptures in the Wieliczka salt mines

FOOD & DRINK

Of course you can eat extremely good Polish food in Krakow. Yet you can also enjoy the culinary achievements of many other nationalities; the gastronomic world is multifaceted and anything but boring.

It was also true in Socialist days: even then, Krakow had a fine reputation as a culinary stronghold. Today top-quality Polish cuisine means that a great deal of fish (trout and carp) and game are served, crayfish soup, fillet of venison and duck are as much part of the Polish tradition as *pierogi* (stuffed dumplings) and *gołąbki* (cabbage rolls). Polish cooks are also famous for their good soups, *barszcz* (made of beetroots),

żurek (flour soup) and *zupa borowikowa* (boletus mushroom soup) are served in almost all restaurants. The Poles eat a lot of meat – pork and veal, as well as poultry. Lamb is usually served accompanied by potatoes or rice and the traditional groats (crushed grain) in some restaurants. Salad used to be something of a rarity but that has now changed: vegetarians will not be at a loss as to what to eat either – there is even a meatless version of the national dish *pierogi*. Frequently, the atmosphere in the restaurants and cafés – many of which are located in renovated Gothic cellars – adds the crowning touch to what has already been a good, and

Photo: Cherubino Restaurant

No matter whether it is Polish or international cuisine, pizza or *pierogi*, Krakow has a well-deserved reputation for culinary variety

usually not even very expensive, meal. In the summertime, tables are moved outside into romantic inner courtyards and even onto busy streets. That is when Poland's famous Żywiec and Okocim beers taste especially good.

The fact that Krakow has such a diversified culinary scene is due to its history. Kosher and sweet-and-sour dishes come from the Jewish kitchen, the Habsburg period added food from Bohemia, Hungary and Austria – including the lovingly cared for coffee-house culture. In the meantime, Spanish, Asian, Mexican, Greek and Indian food is also available, not to forget the many Italian restaurants. The Polish version of the pizza also makes a tasty snack: *zapiekanka* is a toasted piece of baguette topped with mushrooms, vegetables or ham.

The majority of restaurants, including the best and most expensive, are in the city centre and in Kazimierz. Lunch at around midday is the most important meal of the

phere of a farmhouse parlour. Wonderful salads, the apple cake is famous all over Krakow, home-made liqueurs. 2 minutes from the Market Square in a peaceful side

The Pożegnanie z Afryką Café is a mecca for all lovers of coffee

day; dinner is usually served between 6 and 7pm. Almost all of the restaurants are open until late at night and – unless noted otherwise – every day. Many bistros start serving breakfast at 8am and most of the cafés also sell snacks as well as drinks. Smoking is still allowed in Polish restaurants but there are usually also areas for non-smokers.

CAFÉS & CAKE SHOPS

CAFÉ CAMELOT
(110 C2) (*ØD D4*)
This café was formerly a gallery for folkloric art; the collection of naïve paintings by the Polish artist Nikifor is one of the largest in the country, and the typical wooden cupboards, glass cabinets and hand-painted chests create the atmos-

street. It is also very pleasant to sit outside. *Daily | ul. św. Tomasza 17 | tel. 01 24 21 01 23*

CAFÉ MANGGHA ☆ (113 D4) (*ØD C8*)
On the premises of the Japanese Museum with a superb view of Wawel Hill from the terrace. Wide variety of teas **INSIDER TIP** served in traditional Japanese clay pots and small cups, Japanese beer and sourcherry tart. *Closed Mon | ul. Marii Konopnickiej 26 | tel. 01 22 67 27 03 | www.cafe manggha.pl*

JAMA MICHALIKA (110 C2) (*ØD E4*)
One of the oldest cafés (1895) in the city and still boasting its original Art Nouveau interior. At the beginning of the 20th century, many students from the art academy came here and 'paid' their bills with their paintings. Snacks as well as cakes.

Daily | ul. Floriańska 45 | tel. 01 24 22 15 61 | www.jamamichalika.pl

KAWIARNIA NOWOROLSKI
(110 B3) *(ₘ D5)*

You should take your time and try one of the delicious cakes in this traditional, chic Viennese-style café: we especially recommend the **INSIDER TIP** gateau made with three different kinds of chocolate. You can also sit outside directly on the Market Square with a view of St Mary's Church. *Daily from 8am | Rynek Główny 1/3 | tel. 01 24 22 47 71 | www.noworolski.com.pl*

NOWA PROWINCJA **(110 B3)** *(ₘ D5)*

A cult café in the heart of town. Have a cup of chocolate to go along with the sweet things such as the chocolate cake and lemon tart. There is a room for non-smokers on the first floor and you sit on old school benches outside. *Daily | ul. Bracka 3–5 | tel. 01 24 30 24 66 | www.nowaprowincja.krakow.pl*

POŻEGNANIE Z AFRYKĄ
(110 C3) *(ₘ E4)*

This is a very special address for caffeine lovers: Countless varieties of coffee are served and sold here. They even have a supply of the world's most exclusive and expensive coffee – Kopi Luwak from Indonesia – of which only 300–400kg (660–880lbs) are produced each year. *Daily | ul. św. Tomasza 21 | tel. 01 24 21 23 39 | www.pozegnanie.pl*

SŁODKI WENTZL **(110 B3)** *(ₘ D5)*

This is where you will find the largest selection of desserts in Krakow; from simple cakes and lavish gateaux to exquisite ice-cream creations. It is especially enjoyable to sit outside and enjoy the view of the Cloth Hall. You can also take away ice cream. *Daily | Rynek Główny 19 | tel. 01 24 29 57 12 | www.slodkiwentzl.pl*

ICE CREAM PARLOURS

GRYCAN **(115 D–E 2–3)** *(ₘ H7)*

This family-run business has sold ice cream for over 80 years; it sells more than 40 different varieties of ice cream and many types of sorbet; try the orange liqueur, rose and truffle varieties. *Daily | ul. Podgórska 34 (Galeria Kazimierz) | tel. 01 24 33 01 53 | www.grycan.pl*

INSIDER TIP PRACOWNIA CUKIERNICZA STANISŁAW SARGA **(114 C3)** *(ₘ G8)*

This mini-shop only sells six kinds of ice cream – but maybe that is exactly why it is the best in town. Chocolate ice cream with great chunks of chocolate and strawberry ice cream with whole strawberries – fantastic! The only problem; you might have to queue up a while to be served. *Closed Sun | ul. Starowiślna 83 | tram 13: św. Wawrzyńca*

MARCO POLO HIGHLIGHTS

⭐ **Chimera**
Enormous selection of fresh salads – in the charming inner courtyard or in front of the fire → p. 56

⭐ **Wesele**
Polish cooking with international flair → p. 58

⭐ **Carlito**
Polish and Italian cooking served with a view from the rooftop terrace → p. 58

⭐ **Wentzl**
Absolute luxury and unique game dishes in one of the best restaurants in Krakow → p. 58

LOCAL SPECIALITIES

▶ **Barszcz** – soup of beetroots, with egg, potatoes or croquettes. Also a typical Christmas meal with small dumplings stuffed with sauerkraut (photo left)
▶ **Bigos** – meat, sausage, sauerkraut and mushroom stew. The luxury version is served with red wine (photo right)
▶ **Gołąbki** – cabbage leaves stuffed with a filling of rice and meat; a vegetarian version with rice and mushrooms is also common. Served in tomato or mushroom sauce

▶ **Pierogi** – large dumplings with a variety of fillings. *Pierogi ruskie:* with boiled potatoes and curd cheese, *pierogi z mięsem:* with meat, *pierogi z kapustą i grzybami:* with sauerkraut and mushrooms. In season, also with strawberries *(z truskawkami)* or plums *(z śliwkami)*
▶ **Rosół** – meat bouillon with noodles, usually served on Sunday
▶ **Sernik** – cheesecake
▶ **Żurek** – sour flour soup with boiled egg, sausage and potatoes

SNACK BARS

CAFÉ BOTANICA (110 B4) (*ω D5*)
Coffee and cake and a wide selection of salads, tarts, toasts and sandwiches. There is an attractive INSIDERTIP orangery with a glass roof in the courtyard. *Daily | ul. Bracka 9 | tel. 01 24 22 89 80 | www.cafe botanica.pl*

CHIMERA ⭐ (110 B3) (*ω D5*)
A small serving of the salads you can put together according to your own wishes at the bar costs 4 Pln; a large one, 6 Pln. There is a garden in summer and a fireplace in winter. In addition nettle juice, grilled food and soups. *Daily noon–11pm |*
ul. św. Anny 13 | tel. 01 22 92 12 12 | www. chimera.com.pl

DYNIA (108 C4) (*ω C4*)
Tasty snacks: breakfast, lunch and dinner. Good choice of salads and a 'fitness menu'. Lovely garden in the courtyard in summer. *Mon–Fri 8am–10pm, Sat/Sun 9am–10pm | ul. Krupnicza 20 | tel. 01 24 30 08 38 | www.dynia.krakow.pl*

GREEN WAY ☺ (110 C3) (*ω E5*)
There is a lot of action at midday in this vegetarian, organic bar with gluten-free, fair-trade products *(set lunch from 15 Pln)*. Especially good: milkshakes, carrot cake and *kwas chlebowy,* a drink produced us-

ing wholemeal bread. *Mon–Fri 10am–10pm, Sat/Sun 11am–9pm | ul. Mikołajska 14 | tel. 01 24 31 10 27 | www.greenway.pl*

INSIDER TIP ▶ PIEROŻKI U VINCENTA
(114 A–B3) (*ØØ E8*)

More than 30 different kinds of *pierogi*. Try *kreplach* (dough dumplings with meat, potatoes or cabbage), a Jewish speciality, and *pielmieni,* a Russian delicacy stuffed with meat. *Daily | ul. Bożego Ciała 12 | tel. 01 24 30 68 34 | tram 8: pl. Wolnica*

PIZZERIAS

BANOLLI (114 B4) (*ØØ F9*)

Restaurant with a modern, unfussy interior for young people. Very inexpensive pizzas, delivery service and many special offers: for example, the second pizza costs 60 percent less. Several branches. *Daily | pl. Wolnica 10 | tel. 01 24 32 11 22 | tram 8: pl. Wolnica*

TRZY PAPRYCZKI (110 B4) (*ØØ D6*)

Rustically decorated restaurant with Italian flair and more than 20 different kinds of pizza. Also antipasti, grilled meat, pasta and salads. *Daily | ul. Poselska 17 | tel. 01 22 92 55 32 | www.trzypapryczki.krakow.pl*

RESTAURANTS: EXPENSIVE

ANCORA ☆ (110 C4) (*ØØ D5*)

Fusion of traditional and modern cuisine. Fantastic ambience with a view of the Dominican Church. Some of the combinations may seem a bit unusual at first, but you must try them: herring in boletus sauce or chocolate soufflé with blue cheese. More than 400 wines. *Daily | ul. Dominikańska 3 | tel. 01 24 30 20 45 | www.ancora-restaurant.com*

CYRANO DE BERGERAC (110 B2) (*ØØ D4*)

Elegant restaurant in a Gothic cellar serving mainly French food: Lamb chops with rosemary or fillet of venison. Good selection of international wines. *Closed Sun | ul. Sławkowska 26 | tel. 01 24 29 54 20 | www.cyranodebergerac.pl*

FARINA (110 C2) (*ØØ E4*)

The best fish restaurant in Krakow serves INSIDER TIP ▶ freshly-caught seafood from Thursday to Sunday. The menu also offers dishes for those who do not wish to eat fish. *Daily | ul. św. Marka 31 | tel. 01 24 22 16 80 | www.farina.krakow.pl*

HAWEŁKA – RESTAURACJA TETMAJEROWSKA (110 B3) (*ØØ D5*)

This restaurant has served exclusive Polish and international cuisine in an original fin-de-siècle ambience since 1876. The staircase is adorned with paintings by the Polish Art Nouveau artists Wyspiański, Tetmajer and Stanisławski. Wide choice of game dishes and fish. There is a slightly less expensive version of the restaurant on the ground floor with a very special bole-

LOW BUDGET

▶ There is often a lunchtime *menu of the day (danie dnia),* which is a lot less expensive than the dishes on the evening menu. *From 15 Pln*

▶ The *milk bars (bar mleczny)* are especially popular with students Soups, salads and simple meat dishes for the not-so-well-off, *e.g.: Bar pod Temidą | ul. Grodzka 43*

▶ The cheapest and quickest way to satisfy your hunger will take you to ul. Floriańska and ul. Grodzka. There, you will find loads of *kebab stands;* vegetarian ones too. *From 10 Pln*

tus mushroom soup served in bread on the menu. The *Hawełka Cake Shop* in the entrance passage offers sweet things to take away. *Daily mid-March–mid-Nov from 11am, at other times noon–10.30pm, restaurant on the first floor, on demand (min. 10 guests) | Rynek Główny 34 | tel. 0124 22 63 24 | www.hawelka.pl*

SZARA (110 B3) (*ΩΩ D5*)

Restaurant in a medieval town house with Gothic arches and Art Nouveau frescoes. Luxurious international cooking: *raraka* (potato pancakes with caviar, sour cream and onions), reindeer tartare with horseradish and salmon tartare with capers. **INSIDERTIP** A less expensive lunch is served between noon and 3pm. There are tables outside in summer with a wonderful view of the illuminated St Mary's Church in the evening and a second room with a bar serving excellent cocktails. *Daily 11am–11pm | Rynek Główny 6 | tel. 0609 54 46 29 | www.szara.pl*

WESELE ★ (110 C4) (*ΩΩ D5*)

This restaurant with a view of the Market Square serves modern Polish and Italian cooking on two floors – great combinations such as Polish potato pancakes with sour cream and duck with pears in honey. *Daily noon–11pm | Rynek Główny 10 | tel. 0124 22 74 60 | www.weselerestauracja.pl*

RESTAURANTS: MODERATE

CARLITO ★ ✅ (110 C3) (*ΩΩ E4*)

One of the best Italian restaurants. The tomato and green pea soup, *gnocchi peperoncino* and meat dishes are especially tasty. Rooftop terrace with beautiful view. *Daily | ul. Floriańska 28 | tel. 0124 29 19 12 | www.restauracjacarlito.pl*

CHERUBINO (110 C2) (*ΩΩ E4*)

In this restaurant, Italian and Polish meat and fish dishes are prepared absolutely fresh in a large wood-burning oven over an open fire. Rustic ambience. *Daily | ul. św. Tomasza 15 | tel. 0124 29 40 07 | www.cherubino.pl*

CHŁOPSKIE JADŁO (114 A3) (*ΩΩ D4*)

The country-style version of Polish cuisine: heavy and fat but still really delicious. The restaurant has the ambience of an old

GOURMET RESTAURANTS

Wentzl ★ ● ✅ (110 B3) (*ΩΩ D5*)

Wentzl has been one of the best restaurants in Krakow for over 200 years. The Gothic town house is located directly in the Market Square. Reserve a table near a window; the view is fantastic. The game dishes are to be recommended. Extensive wine list. *Main course with meat (duck, veal) or fish from 56 Pln | daily | Rynek Główny 19 | tel. 0124 29 57 12 | www.wentzl.pl*

Wierzynek ✅ (110 B3) (*ΩΩ D5*)

If legends are to be believed, kings were already dining in this famous restaurant in the 14th century. The three-storey establishment serves Polish and international specialities; the best places are next to the windows with a view over the Market Square. Reservations are essential in the evening. *Main courses from 52 Pln | daily 1pm–midnight | Rynek Główny 15 | tel. 0124 2 49 00 | www.wierzynek.com.pl*

room in the countryside. Bread and dripping with sour pickles is served as an appetizer and after that you should treat yourself to escalope of pork with plums and garlic or one of the other specialities. *Daily | ul. św. Agnieszki 1 | tel. 01 24 21 85 20 | www.chlopskiejadlo.pl*

KLEZMER HOIS ● (114 C2) (*ற F8*)

A Jewish (but not fully kosher) restaurant in the building that used to house the ritual bath. (You can see the remains of the pool in the cellar.) The restaurant is furnished like a bourgeois dining room from the early 20th century with old dark furniture and embroidered tablecloths. The speciality of the house: turkey in honey sauce. There are often klezmer concerts at the weekend. *Daily | ul. Szeroka 6 | tel. 01 24 11 12 45 | www.klezmer.pl | tram 13: ul. Miodowa*

POD ANIOŁAMI (110 B4) (*ற D6*)

Grilled meat, pies (hare pie with cranberries), and duck with apple accompanied by dark wholemeal bread, red cabbage and sour pickles: the best the Polish kitchen has to offer served in a Gothic cellar or in a small courtyard garden in summer. Good wine list and Polish mead. *Daily | ul. Grodzka 35 | tel. 01 24 21 39 99 | www.podaniolami.pl*

RESTAURANTS: BUDGET

GOSPODA KOKO (110 B3) (*ற D5*)

This simply decorated inn serves good square Polish meals. Set lunch with homemade stewed fruit from 12 Pln. *Daily. | ul. Gołębia 8 | tel. 01 24 30 21 35*

GRUZIŃSKIE CHACZAPURI

These restaurants focus on the highlights of Georgian cooking, such as grilled meat with rice and various sauces. Specialities: *lavasz* (spicy meat in a kind of tortilla),

Hospitality for more than 200 years: Wentzl Restaurant

inhali (large dumplings stuffed with raw meat and then boiled). In addition, special servings for children and good wines from Georgia. *Daily | ul. Floriańska 26 (110 C2) (ற E4) | tel. 012 4 29 11 31; ul. Sienna 4 (110 B–C3) (ற E5) | tel. 012 4 29 11 66; ul. Św. Anny 4 (110 A–B3) (ற D5) | tel. 01 24 22 61 28 | www.chaczapuri.pl*

KOLANKO NUMER 6 (114 B3) (*ற F8*)

This is the place to enjoy all kinds of pancakes in peaceful surroundings: savoury with spinach and feta cheese, meat with curry, apples and onions, or sweet with curd cheese and vanilla sauce. *Daily | ul. Józefa 17 | tel. 01 22 92 03 20 | tram 8: pl. Wolnica*

POLAKOWSKI (114 B2) (*ற F7*)

A self-service restaurant with homemade Polish food. There is a wide selection of soups and meat dishes. *Daily | ul. Miodowa 39 | tel. 01 24 21 07 76*

SHOPPING

CITY **WHERE TO START?**
Besides the **Galeria Krakowsa** and **Galeria Kazimierz**, the most popular shopping areas are on **ul. Floriańska** and **ul. Grodzka**. This is where you will find fashion, shoe and jewellery shops as well as art galleries and antique dealers. There are many souvenir shops in and around the **Rynek Główny**, too, and you will also find an original style of jewellery and out-of-the-ordinary souvenirs on **ul. Józefa** (trams 6 and 8: Plac Wolnica) in Kazimierz.

The brands and chains that have left their mark on all other major cities in the world have also opened their doors in Krakow. However, shopping here still offers surprises, and you will have great fun exploring the smaller shops in the city's beautiful Old Town.

Most of the shops line the Market Square and Royal Way, ul. Floriańska and ul. Grodzka. This is where you will find all of those things that make a shopping spree so much fun. The delicatessen shops, fashion boutiques, art and bric-a-brac offer a wide variety of things you can take home as souvenirs. Equally interesting, although of a different character, are the many small

The flair of a time-honoured trading centre continues to make rummaging and shopping a very special experience in Krakow

modern art galleries, designer jewellery shops and the popular Sunday flea market in Kazimierz. There are no restrictions on opening hours in Poland, so you can shop till you drop *(general opening hours see: Travel Tips)*. If you are on the lookout for something unique, you will probably find it in one of the amber jewellery galleries. Poland is also well-known for its schnapps including *Żybrówka* vodka, *Krupnik (honey*

liqueur) and *Żołądkowa gorzka (bitters)*. Children will be happy to receive a Wawel dragon or traditional wooden toys.

BOOKS

BONA ★ ●
(110 B5) *(ᗰ D6)*

Much more than just a bookshop! In addition to an excellent selection of post-

You will find modern Polish art for your living room at home in the Galeria Gołogórski

cards, illustrated books and guidebooks on the city (also in English), you will also be able to enjoy a good cup of coffee or tea and a piece of cake. If the weather is fine, you can sit at one of the tables outside – with a spectacular view of the Church of Saints Peter and Paul. *Mon–Fri 9am–7pm, Sat 10am–3pm | ul. Kanonicza 11 | www. bonamedia.pl*

PASAŻ HETMAŃSKI
(110 B3) *(ȼ D5)*
You will discover a rich selection of books about Krakow, postcards and stamps, as well as fashion and souvenir articles, in this passageway next to a medieval town house. *Rynek Główny 13*

DELICATESSEN

KREDENS KRAKOWSKI
(110 B4) *(ȼ D5)*
Since 1906, this has been a top address for bread, sausage specialities, jam, honey, tea and sweets. All the articles are traditionally packaged and make original souvenirs. *Ul. Grodzka 7 | krakowskikredens.pl*

SHOPPING CENTRES

GALERIA KAZIMIERZ ●
(115 D–E3) *(ȼ H7)*
Old bricks from buildings that formerly stood on the site were integrated into the new construction of this particularly impressive shopping centre in Krakow. More than 100 shops, cafés, restaurants and a multiplex cinema. *Mon–Sat 10am–10pm, Sun 10am–8pm | ul. Podgórska 34 | www. galeriakazimierz.pl | tram 9, 11, 13: św. Wawrzyńca, then a 5-minute walk along the Vistula*

GALERIA KRAKOWSKA (111 D1) *(ȼ F3)*
There are more than 270 shops selling brand-name sports, fashion and cosmetic articles on the around 390,000 ft² of floor space of this shopping centre, as well as cafés and restaurants. *Mon–Sat 9am–10pm, Sun 10am–9pm | ul. Pawia 5 | www. galeria-krakowska.pl*

PASAŻ HANDLOWY 13 (110 B3) *(ȼ D5)*
This exclusive, multi-storey department store on the Market Square is a successful

combination of Gothic and Renaissance architecture with a modern construction of metal and glass. It provides an ambience that is just as perfect for brands such as Benetton, Sisley, Diesel and Cerutti, as it is for INSIDER TIP exclusive delicatessen from around the world and a large selection of Italian wines. *Rynek Główny 13*

CHILDREN

INSIDER TIP BAJO ☺
(110 B6) (*₥ D7*)

A cult address for (ecologically sound) wooden toys, the products ranging from tiny figures and cars to wooden horses and doll's prams. The beautiful finger puppets in gorgeous clothes are made in Krakow. *Ul. Grodzka 60 | bajo.eu*

BUKOWSKI (110 B3) (*₥ D5*)

The youngsters will think they are in heaven: 400 small and large plush teddies and other soft toys in old wooden cupboards reaching from the floor to the ceiling. *Tue–Sat 10am–7pm, Sun/Mon 10am–6pm | ul. Sienna 1 | galeriabukowski.pl*

ART GALLERIES

GALERIA GOŁOGÓRSKI
(110 B4) (*₥ D6*)

The gallery run by the artist Marian Gołogórski specialises in modern Polish painting and sculptures made of metal, stone and glass. *Ul. Grodzka 29 | gologorskigallery.blogspot.com*

JAN FEJKIEL GALLERY (110 B5) (*₥ D7*)

This gallery has the largest stock of modern Polish graphic art and drawings in the city. It places great importance on supporting young Krakow artists and organises many exhibitions. *Mon–Fri 11am–6pm, Sat 11am–3pm | ul. Grodzka 65 | www.fejkielgallery.com*

SOPOCKI DOM AUKCYJNY
(110 B3) (*₥ D4*)

Antiques, fine china, jewellery. The old Polish paintings offered for sale are particularly interesting. *Rynek Główny 45 | www.sda.pl*

SZALOM (114 B3) (*₥ F8*)

The top gallery in Kazimierz. Modern Polish and Israeli artists, ceramics and fascinating jewellery. *Ul. Józefa 16*

FASHION

OUTLET (109 E5) (*₥ D5*)

Brand-name clothing, shoes, bags and underwear from companies such as Mango, Esprit, Hugo Boss and Palmers with prices

---

MARCO POLO HIGHLIGHTS

★ **Bona**
The address for bookworms and coffee connoisseurs. Beautifully illustrated books about Krakow and Poland → p. 61

★ **Simple**
Modern and classic fashion, individually designed and produced in extremely limited numbers – a guarantee that you will be the only one wearing the dress at the party! → p. 64

★ **Ambra Stile**
Remarkable jewellery – and not just in amber. If you look carefully, you might be lucky and find something completely unique → p. 64

★ **Wedel**
Handmade chocolates, drinking chocolate and mouth-watering desserts – pure heaven! → p. 65

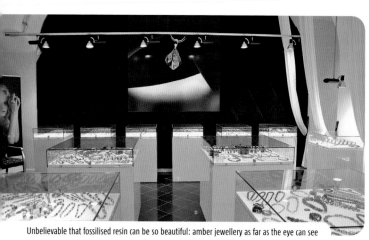

Unbelievable that fossilised resin can be so beautiful: amber jewellery as far as the eye can see

reduced by as much as 70 percent. *Ul. sw. Anny (entrance on ul. Wiślna)*

SIMPLE ★ (110 B4) *(ɯ D5)*
Two Polish designers sell classic fashion for ladies but with a modern note; lovely summer and evening dresses and elegant suits. Very exclusive; only two or three pieces of each model are made. *Ul. Grodzka 18 | www.simple-cp.com*

JEWELLERY

A&S
Here you will find amber jewellery, spoons, chess games and cuff links. A&S only sells genuine natural amber (with a certificate of authenticity). Jewellery made out of INSIDER TIP striped flint from Sandomierz makes a very special souvenir. *Ul. Sienna 1 (110 C3) (ɯ D5) | ul. Grodzka 29 (110 B4) (ɯ D6)*

AMBRA STILE ★ (110 B5) *(ɯ D6)*
Italian silver jewellery with semi-precious stones, as well as jewellery with amber and locally made pieces – from cuff links to small ants and lizards with amber bodies.

Mon–Sat 11am–8pm | ul. Grodzka 45 | www.ambrastile.krakow.pl

BLAZKO JEWELLERY (114 B3) *(ɯ F8)*
Silver jewellery with a black-and-white finish is the extremely attractive hallmark of Grzegorz Błażko's gallery. *Ul. Józefa 11 | www.blazko.pl*

SHOES & BAGS

DE MEHLEM (110 B4) *(ɯ D6)*
Handmade bags and leather clothing have been sold in this shop since 1912. They also stock bags with amber appliqués made by the Polish Batycki Company. *Ul. Grodzka 43 | www.demehlem.com*

GINO ROSSI (110 B3) *(ɯ D4)*
Trendy, Italian-style shoes and bags of the finest leather for all the family. *There are several branches, e.g. Ul. Szewska 4 | www.ginorossi.com*

WITTCHEN (115 E3) *(ɯ H7)*
Leather bags, cases, gloves, luggage, jackets and umbrellas. *Ul. Podgórska 34 | Gal. Kazimierz | www.wittchen.com*

SOUVENIRS

BROKAT
(110 B3) (*D5*)
Exquisite fabric articles: angels, dolls, hand-made cushions and tea cosies. Also many pieces made by the students of the Krakow art academy. *Rynek Główny*

GALERIA
(110 B5) (*D7*)
Small glass, ceramic, pottery and wooden souvenirs; most of them handmade by Krakow artists. The hand-painted furniture is particularly appealing. *Ul. Grodzka 60*

GALERIA D'ART NAIV
(114 B3) (*F8*)
Traditional naïve art such as stained glass, wooden sculptures, and paintings. The owner has the largest collection of this kind of art in Poland. *Ul. Józefa 11*

SUKIENNICE (CLOTH HALL)
(110 B3) (*D5*)
The largest selection of souvenirs from Krakow; jewellery, wooden articles, leather bags, traditional clothing, ceramics and glass. *Rynek Główny 2*

SPIRITS

R7 (110 B3) (*D5*)
Here, you will not only be able to stock up on hard spirits but also sweets, cigarettes and cigars. *Rynek Główny 7*

SZAMBELAN (110 B4) (*D5*)
This shop has a fine assortment of spirits and vodka, as well as vinegar and olive oil in enormous bottles. You can sample the spirits on the premises and then have a bottle filled with the amount you want. Try the rose and orange-chocolate liqueurs as well. *Mon–Sat 10am–8pm, Sun 11am–6pm | ul. Gołębia 2 | www.szambelan.pl*

SWEETS

TORUŃSKIE PIERNIKI
(110 B4) (*D5*)
The famous gingerbread from Thorn coated with chocolate or with different coloured icing is available in all sizes. *Ul. Grodzka 14*

WAWEL (110 B3) (*D5*)
Chocolate and a large selection of specially packed sweets. Speciality: *śliwki w czekoladzie* – plums in chocolate. *Rynek Główny 32*

WEDEL ★ (110 B3) (*D4*)
The parent company of this chain of pastry shops has sold handmade chocolates and sweets in Warsaw since 1851. Specialities: *torcik wedlowski* (a gateau with layers of chocolate and nut cream) and *ptasie mleczko* (milk chocolates truffles filled with cream). You can sample the delicacies in the café next door. *Daily 9am–10pm | Rynek Główny 46 | wedelpijalnie.pl*

LOW BUDGET

▶ A flea market is held every Sunday in the suburb of *Grzegórzki* (food market during the week). Here you will find all kinds of goods – from old radios to Meissen porcelain. *Ul. Grzegórzecka | tram 1: Hala Targowa.*

▶ *Reserved* sells young fashion for him and her along with inexpensive bags, shoes and costume jewellery. Sales are held several times a year with discounts of up to 70 percent. *Mon–Fri 10am–8pm, Sat 10am–7pm, Sun 10am–5pm | ul. Floriańska 43 | www.reserved.com*

ENTERTAINMENT

WHERE TO START?

Krakow's coolest jazz venues are below ground level in the medieval cellars, while the best clubs and pubs line the streets around the **Rynek Główny**. Most of them are in the pedestrian precinct. Klezmer music is played in many of the Jewish restaurants on ul. Szeroka in **Kazimierz**. The **Plac Nowy** is where the young crowd gets together to have fun. Tram number 13 (ul. Midowa) takes you directly to Kazimierz's nightlife.

Opera or drama, jazz or klezmer, cinema, a concert or club. There are not many other cities where the nightlife is as varied and exciting as it is in Krakow – and where the city has managed to retain its own unique atmosphere.

The Krakow Philharmonic Hall, the many theatres and opera house all guarantee entertainment of a very high standard. The same applies to classical venues held outdoors or at special locations: in the arcaded courtyard of the Wawel Castle, for example, or at one of the concerts of religious or secular music in the many churches in the city. The churches are usually not heated so you should always

No matter whether you prefer classical music, disco, jazz or klezmer, outdoors or in a Gothic cellar: there is something for every taste

make sure that you have a light pullover with you – even in summer. However, Krakow is mainly famous for its jazz concerts. The exceptional violinist Nigel Kennedy lives here for that reason and often appears in jazz clubs in addition to his regular concerts in the Philharmonic Hall. Many of the pubs and clubs are not only music venues but also restaurants and you can even dance in some of them: there are no strict divisions. Most of the pubs are underground in beautifully renovated cellars and many have an inner courtyard or garden.

The trendiest and newest places are all in Kazimierz. The entire area around the Plac Nowy is full of cafés, clubs and pubs in old – often not completely renovated – residential buildings and cellars. There is often a jumble of chairs that do not match,

Live concerts strike the right note in Showtime, the largest music club in the city

old sofas, cinema chairs and school benches – the atmosphere in Kazimierz, with its good music and young crowd, guarantees that the fun continues until the early hours of the morning. It all comes with an artistic touch: many of the locations organise exhibitions of works by young artists or modern theatre and cabaret performances. Night owls will find things are a little more sophisticated at the addresses in the centre of town than in trendy Kazimierz where the nightlife is more varied and chaotic, and rarely stops before dawn. In the old part of town, it is more likely that you will be asked for an ID or turned away by a bouncer for not being properly dressed.

Most of the clubs and pubs are easy to reach on foot and are in the area around the Rynek Główny. Women do not usually have to pay an entrance fee, but men are normally charged 20–30 Pln to get in. However, late at night (after 1am), there is free admission for everybody in most of the clubs. You should not take too many valuables or any more money than you need when you set off in the evening; at the weekend, there is usually a lot of activity in the clubs and that is accompanied by a lot of pushing and shoving. Some clubs demand guests are a minimum age of 21, and there is a strict rule at all locations: no alcohol and cigarettes if you are under 18! Krakow also has a number of lovely little cinemas where films are shown in the original language with Polish subtitles.

CLUBS & DISCOS

PROZAK
(110 B–C4) (*ш D5*)
A typical Krakow disco in a cellar, with three dance floors, four bars and red-and-blue neon lights. This is a very popular location with the young crowd who have fun dancing to music played by exceptionally good DJs: funk, disco, electro, house. *Daily from 6pm | pl. Dominkański 6 | www. prozak.pl*

PRZYCHODNIA TOWARZYSKA
(110 C2) (*ш E4*)
Here, people do not only dance on the three floors but also on the top of the enormously long bar, which has 88 drawers and looks a bit like something out of a chemist's shop. Translated, the name

of the club is 'Service to Save Society'; its special drink is called *Antidotum* and supposedly helps combat boredom. The theme parties, such as the Ibiza Party, at which guests are expected to show up in swimming gear, also take care of that. The bouncers make sure that guests are properly dressed. *Mon–Sat from 6pm | ul. Floriańska 53 | www.przychodnia-towarzyska.pl*

REAKTYWACJA
(110 B4) *(🗺 D6)*
Dance and music club in a cellar and on the first floor. People chill out here every day, but they also dance to house and techno, and there are special events such as karaoke and reggae nights. During happy hour on Monday and Wednesday *(4–6pm)*, a large beer only costs 3 Pln. Do not go too casually dressed, otherwise the bouncer might not let you in! *Daily from 6pm | ul. Grodzka 34 | www.reaktywacja.com.pl*

ROENTGEN (110 B2) *(🗺 D4)*
Simply decorated but with excellent music *(Thu–Sat)* played by the best DJs: house, minimal or drum'n'bass. Minimum age 21. *Daily from 3pm | pl. Szczepański 3*

SHOWTIME (110 B3) *(🗺 D5)*
With room for 300 guests, Showtime is the largest music and dance club in the city. **INSIDER TIP** Fantastic view of the Cloth Hall. There is a small pub in the first room and either live concerts are held *(from 9.30pm)* or people can dance to canned music in

MARCO POLO HIGHLIGHTS

★ Harris Piano Jazz Bar
Jazz is jazz is jazz: musicians from all spheres of jazz take their place on the stage of one of the most popular clubs in town several nights a week → p. 70

★ Piano Rouge
Not only the interior – complete with red carpet – is luxurious. The music and Indian cuisine are also top class → p. 71

★ Baraka
Set off for the future inside this spaceship (but do not forget your drink) → p. 72

★ Alchemia
One of Krakow's cult locations in the epicentre of the dynamic nightlife in Kazimierz: a stuffed crocodile over the bar, no electric light, old furniture, unplastered walls and apple cake to die for! → p. 72

★ Filharmonia Krakowska im. Karola Szymanowskiego
Symphonies, organ and jazz concerts: one of the best orchestras in the country, named after the composer Karol Szymanowski who died in 1937, has a virtuoso command of all styles of music → p. 73

the three large rooms: pop, rock, and funk. *Daily 6pm–4am | Rynek Główny 28*

STALOWE MAGNOLIE
(110 C2) (*m D4*)
Serves good drinks and looks like a club for insiders: you have to ring the doorbell to get in. Once you cross the threshold, you will discover the flair of the fin-de-siècle atmosphere: dim lighting and comfy sofas and four-poster beds to sit on. Friday and Saturday are the nights for dancing; there are concerts during the week and on Sunday *(from 10pm). Classy crowd. Daily*

JAZZ

HARRIS PIANO JAZZ BAR ★ ●
(110 B3) (*m D4*)
If you drop in here, you will have hit on one of the most popular jazz clubs in Krakow. There are several live concerts every week *(from 9pm)*: traditional jazz on Tuesday, a jam session on Thursday, Friday is blues night and international jazz stars perform on Saturday. Good drinks and a fine selection of beer are served at one of the longest bars in town *Daily 9pm–2am | Rynek Główny 28 | www.harris.krakow.pl*

Harris Piano Jazz Bar plays jazz, jazz and more jazz

from 6pm | ul. šw. Jana 15 | www.stalowe magnolie.com

VOODOO MUSIC CLUB
(110 C3) (*m E4*)
A futuristically-decorated club in old Gothic cellar rooms: the glass walls have violet-coloured lighting, and you can relax on large leather sofas. DJs blast the dance floor with disco, funk and pop. *Daily from 6pm, happy hour 6–8pm | ul. Floriańska 6*

INDIGO (110 C2) (*m E4*)
Jazz venue for a sophisticated audience in rooms in a cellar. Black-and-white photographs on the walls, a large wooden bar, very extensive drink list. Starting at 9pm, there are live jazz and rock concerts on the stage in the main room. Next to it, there is a room with a gigantic screen for those more interested in watching football. *Mon–Fri from 2pm, Sat/Sun from 4pm | ul. Floriańska 26*

PIANO ROUGE ⭐ (110 B3) *(🚇 D5)*

This jazz club pampers its guests with its luxurious interior decoration with red carpets, chandeliers and cosy sofas. Not only excellent live jazz is on the menu here *(from 9 or 10pm) though*, you can still any pangs of hunger you feel: the club serves a variety of Indian and Polish specialities. *Daily from 11am | Rynek Główny 46 | www. thepianorouge.com*

PIEC ART (110 B3) *(🚇 D4)*

You can listen to jazz concerts every Wednesday and Thursday at 8.30pm in this magnificently renovated Gothic cellar, and eat and drink well at the same time. The speciality is fish soup and there is also a long list of drinks and cocktails. The bar was built into a huge, partly tiled oven. That gave the club its name: *piec* is Polish for oven, furnace or hearth. Top Polish artists consider it an honour to play here where they alternate with international stars. Minimum age 21. *Daily from 3pm | ul. Szewska 21 | www.piecart.pl*

CINEMAS

ARS ●
(110 B2) *(🚇 D4)*

Five auditoriums under a single roof, including INSIDER TIP a cinema café *(kiniarnia)*, in which you can order drinks from the bar while the film is showing. Particularly impressive: the *Reduta* in an old ballroom. The films are shown in the original language. *Ul. św. Jana 6 | www. ars.pl*

POD BARANAMI
(110 B3) *(🚇 D5)*

The three air-conditioned auditoriums are located in a former palace directly on the Market Square. The cinema organises INSIDER TIP programmes on special themes several times each year. This might include a week of Spanish or African films, although the main focus is on European cinema. Original versions of the films are screened. *Rynek Główny 27 (Pałac Pod Baranami) | www.kinopodbaranami.pl*

RELAX & ENJOY

City trips can be rather tiring, and it is therefore a good idea to take a break from time to time. A *paddle-boat tour on the Vistula (May–mid-Sept daily 10am to nightfall | 20–30 Pln/hour| ul. Kościuszki 16)* **(112 B2)** *(🚇 B7)* has two wonderful effects: you will experience Krakow from a completely new perspective – and be able to really relax on the water on a warm, sunny day. Relaxation is also what ● *Kryspinów (entrance fee 7 Pln, parking 5 Pln | www.kryspinow.com.pl | bus 209: Kryspinów Zalew)* **(117 D4)** *(🚇 0)* is all about. That is where you will be able to enjoy yourself swimming, rowing, wind-surfing or just splashing around in the artificial lakes in the green countryside only 18km (11mi) west of Krakow on the A4. And the ● *Farmona Wellness & Spa (Mon 2–9pm, Tue–Fri 10am–9pm, Sat/ Sun 9am–10pm | ul. Jugowicka 10c | tel. 01 22 52 70 20 | www.spakrakow.pl | bus 244: Jugowicka)* **(117 E5)** *(🚇 0)* in the hotel of the same name is a genuine feel-good oasis. Regardless of whether you are alone or with a partner, you will be pampered all day long with special treatments from Bali and Hawaii: massages with hot stones and fragrant oils followed by aromatic baths.

PUBS & INNS

ALCHEMIA ★ (114 B3) (*ⅢΩ F8*)
Cult pub in Kazimierz: There is a stuffed crocodile hanging over the bar and guests enter the next room through a cupboard. There is no electric light inside, only candles, and you sit on wobbly chairs at old tables. The drinks more than make up for this though, and the apple cake is absolutely sensational. Concerts and modern theatre productions are held in the cellar. If you sit outside, you really will be in the heart of Young Kazimierz with its countless pubs and will have an opportunity to observe all the comings and goings on the Plac Nowy. *Daily from 10am | ul. Estery 5 | www.alchemia.com.pl*

BARAKA ★ (114 B3) (*ⅢΩ F8*)
Guests here feel like they are in a futuristic laboratory or spaceship: a lot of metal, red chairs and stools, blue-and-red illuminated bar. Exhibitions of art by young Krakow artists are shown on the second floor from 5pm. *Daily from 10am | corner of pl. Nowy/ul. Warszauera*

CHILL OUT CLUB ●
(110 C2) (*ⅢΩ E4*)
This is the ideal place for all those who want to spend an afternoon or evening relaxing to good music of an acceptable decibel. Excellent drinks and snacks are served to take the edge off your appetite, and occasionally events such as the Winter Disco (a carefree party in the wintery inner courtyard) are organised. The same inner courtyard, with its cosy sofas and swing, is also an inviting place to unwind in summer. *Daily from noon | ul. św. Jana 15*

MIEJSCE (114 B3) (*ⅢΩ F8*)
The interior design of this location, which pays tribute to the flair and atmosphere of the 1960s and 1970s, is what makes the Miejsce so special. The walls are decorated with original posters from the period and they are changed every month. The drink list not only has the usual alcoholic beverages but also some INSIDER TIP absolutely unbelievable creations – such as parsley-flavoured lemonade. *Daily 10am–10pm | ul. Estery 1*

PAPARAZZI
(110 C3) (*ⅢΩ E5*)
The name says it all: there are newspaper cuttings and photos of models and actors from all over the world on the walls, and 'fashion tv' runs non-stop in one of the rooms. *Lunch time* is celebrated from noon until 5pm. Large selection of drinks at low prices. *Mon–Fri 11am–1pm, Sat/Sun 4pm–1am, Mon–Fri 4–8pm Happy Hour | ul. Mikołajska 9 | www.paparazzi.com.pl*

PROPAGANDA
(114 B2) (*ⅢΩ E7*)
This is the place for you if you want to feel real Communist atmosphere: Lenin greets the guests from posters on the walls. Other parts of the wall are covered in socialist-style signs. Many good drinks including INSIDER TIP the speciality of the house: *wściekły pies*, ice-cold vodka with Tabasco and raspberry syrup. *Daily from noon | ul. Miodowa 20*

LOW BUDGET

▶ In most of the *Krakow clubs*, women do not have to pay an entrance fee – or only a reduced one; ● late at night, it is usually free for all.

▶ Many pubs and clubs have *happy-hour days* (often on Monday) when beer is extremely inexpensive.

SINGER (114 B3) (*F8*)

Nomen est omen: Old Singer sewing machines have been turned into the tables of this, the oldest, pub in Kazimierz. You can also sit outside in the fresh air; fine selection of alcoholic drinks, as well as coffee and cake. *Daily from 10am | corner of ul. Izaaka/Estery*

WARSZTAT (114 B3) (*F8*)

A mixture of café and pub. The biggest impression is made by the interior decoration with all the old musical instruments: a piano has been inserted upright into the bar! This is where the way-out in-crowd

this neo-Baroque building since 1930. The Krakow Radio Symphony and Philharmonic Orchestras are two of the best in Poland. Symphonic and organ concerts are held in this hall as are jazz performances and other concerts within the framework of various festivals. Programme in English. The society also organises the *Wieczory wawelskie*, the Wawel Evenings, with programmes of **INSIDER TIP** chamber music in the castle or arcaded courtyard. *Ticket office: Tue–Fri 11am–2pm and 3–5pm, Sat/Sun one hour before the performance | ul. Zwierzyniecka 1 | www.filharmonia. krakow.pl*

Journey back in time to the 1960s and 1970s: homely retro-ambience in the Club Miejsce

meets in Kazimierz. There is laid-back music in the background: blues, jazz or klezmer, and the beer is served in enormous jugs. *Daily from 10am | ul. Izaaka 3*

OPERA & CLASSICAL MUSIC

FILHARMONIA KRAKOWSKA IM. KAROLA SZYMANOWSKIEGO ★
(110 A4) (*C5*)

The Krakow Philharmonic Society was founded in 1909 and has had its home in

OPERA KRAKOWSKA (111 F1) (*H3*)

The opera house presents traditional and modern productions of Polish and international operas. The **INSIDER TIP** Summer Festival is very popular; performances are held in the arcade courtyard of Wawel Castle as well as in the opera house itself. *Ticket office: Mon–Fri 10am–7pm, Sat noon–7pm, Sun two hours before the performance | five price categories between 30 and 120 Pln | ul. Lubicz 48 | www. opera.krakow.pl*

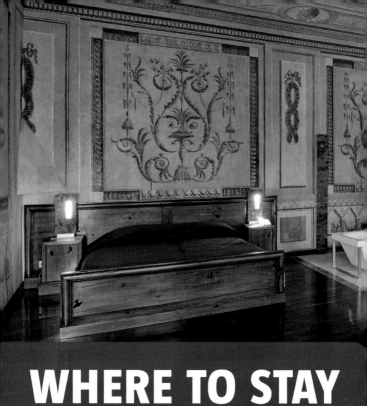

WHERE TO STAY

Most of the well-known international chains operate in Krakow, but there are also absolutely unique, individually designed hotels that will make your stay in the city on the Vistula really special.

The best hotels are located right in the centre in the pedestrian precinct, and most are in Gothic or Renaissance town houses and palaces. They all have their own stories told by the beautifully painted wooden ceilings, Gothic portals and frescoes on the walls – and this rich history is cleverly combined with the modern technology that is standard in this kind of accommodation. Many hotels in the moderate price range are also located in the centre of

town, often quite close to their luxury counterparts. Here, too, guests are assured of comfort and of well-equipped rooms, regardless of whether the hotels are comparatively new and have only been operating for a couple of years or are establishments that have been recently renovated. Krakow's hotel trade has satisfied international standards for a long time.

There are a large number of hotels in the middle category in Kazimierz, too, and this is where you will also find a wide choice of guest houses and private accommodation. In Krakow, the family-run guest houses have a charming atmosphere, even if they

Stylish luxury hotels, Gothic town houses, modern family hotels and cosy guest rooms – such a wide choice is rare!

do not always meet the highest standards. However, the less expensive hotels, frequently in buildings from the 1960s and 1970s, are often miles away from the centre. It is therefore a good idea to choose a better hostel or guest room in a central location – in which you can perhaps prepare your own breakfast – than in a one or two-star hotel away from the city centre.

No matter which hotel you choose, always check to see if there are special offers; there are often price reductions if you stay several nights. In addition, there are often special weekend rates and family offers as well as extras such as city tours and entrance fees to museums, which are included in the price of the room. It is worth taking a look at the individual websites: hotels sometimes offer up to 30 percent discount on online bookings. The high season is from Easter to the end of October; prices are often 50 percent lower in the off-season. You can find special deals for luxury houses under *www.booking.com* and *www.venere.com*. Two good addresses for those looking for hotels or holiday flats are *www.krakow-hotel-guide.com* and *www.krakow-apartments.com*.

restored in some of them. The hotel is in a very quiet area; **INSIDER TIP** the most beautiful rooms are those with a view of ul. Kanonicza, the others overlook the courtyard. There is a spectacular view from the rooftop terrace. If you book via the Internet, you will receive up to 30 percent discount. By the way, there is a reason for the hotel's name: it is said that Copernicus actually

The beauty of Krakow spread out in front of you: the rooftop terrace of the Hotel Copernicus

HOTELS: EXPENSIVE

HOTEL COPERNICUS ✵
(110 B5) (*ID D6*)

Do you fancy a room with a view of the Royal Castle in a listed house from the 16th century? Then, this is the place for you! When the hotel was renovated, great attention was paid to every detail: the rooms are all individually designed and the original Gothic and Renaissance murals were

stayed here when he visited Krakow. *29 rooms | ul. Kanonicza 16 | tel. 01 24 24 34 00 | www.copernicus.hotel.com.pl*

HOTEL GRÓDEK (110 C3) (*ID E5*)

A hotel in a Gothic building in a peaceful location in the heart of town. Each room has a different interior design; the Gothic church floor in the reception area was saved during renovations and laid here. There is a lovely view of the old town from the charming restaurant; the library has a wide selection of books. Objects found during renovation work are displayed in the hotel, in INSIDERTIP Poland's only private archaeological museum. *24 rooms | ul. Na Gródku 4 | tel. 0124 31 90 30 | www.don imirski.com*

OSTOYA PALACE (108 C6) (*∅ B5*)

This stylish hotel, decorated with antique furniture, is located in the renovated, listed Ostaszewski Palace from 1895. It was built by Józef Pokutyński, one of Krakow's best architects. Many details, such as wall paintings and stucco work, were preserved. If you want to sleep in a really big bed (6.6ft × 6.6ft), book one of the suites. *24 rooms | ul. Józefa Piłsudkiego 24 | tel. 0124 30 90 00 | www.ostoyapalace.pl*

PAŁAC BONEROWSKI ★
(110 B3) (*∅ D4*)

Luxurious rooms and suites in a 16th-century castle in a top location directly on the Market Square. Many details, including portals, wooden ceilings and murals, have been preserved. There are two restaurants in the house: *Pod Winogronami* with French and Italian cuisine and *Megami* with Japanese specialities, which is on the top floor under a glass roof. The INSIDERTIP Chopin concerts in the evening are not exclusively reserved for the hotel's guests. *14 rooms | ul. św. Jana 1 | tel. 0123 74 13 00 | www.palacbonerowski.pl*

HOTEL POD RÓŻĄ ★ (110 C2) (*∅ E4*)

The oldest hotel in Krakow: even Honoré de Balzac laid his head here. The original architecture of the 15th-century town house on the Royal Way was combined with the luxury and comfort of the 21st century to create this hotel. Fine restaurant with a large wine cellar. *54 rooms | ul. Floriańska 14 | tel. 0124 24 33 81 | www. hotel.com.pl*

HOTELS: MODERATE

HOTEL ALEF (114 A3) (*∅ E8*)

This hotel in Kazimierz has 35 comfortable, but simply appointed, rooms. The main attraction is the staircase that the owner has turned into an art gallery. There is also a restaurant serving traditional Jewish food. *Ul. św. Agnieszki 5 | tel. 0124 24 31 31 | www.alef.pl*

ATRIUM HOTEL (110 C1) (*∅ E3*)

This modern, centrally located, hotel was renovated just a few years ago. The rooms are simply furnished and there are also two apartments with kitchenettes. *50*

MARCO POLO HIGHLIGHTS

★ Pałac Bonerowski
What more could you ask for: staying in a castle with a view of St Mary's Church and dining on Japanese delicacies under a glass roof → p. 77

★ Hotel Pod Różą
Would you like to sleep in the same room that Balzac slept in? Even that is possible in the oldest hotel in Krakow – here, every night is special → p. 77

★ Pension Trecius
Where the devil spent the night: Centrally located guest house with a pleasantly spine-tingling touch free → p. 81

★ Hotel Stary
Europe's most beautiful hotel also has the most beautiful view of the city from its rooftop terrace → p. 78

rooms | ul. Krzywa 7 | tel. 012 4 30 02 03 | www.hotelatrium.com.pl

APARTAMENTY BRACKA 6
(110 B4) (*ш D5*)

The apartments and studios in this 500-year-old town house in a prime location have been renovated with painstaking care. They all have parquet floors and air-conditioning and some have a balcony. The rooms are equipped with a small kitchenette and wireless Internet access. *8 flats | ul. Bracka 6 | tel. 0608 00 06 09 | www.bracka6.pl*

ELEKTOR HOTEL (110 C2) (*ш E4*)

Stylishly furnished rooms in an old town house in the city centre. The many special offers and arrangements are all part of the hotel's policy; for example, the second room only costs 1 Pln and the third night

is free. Many crowned heads have stayed in these very spacious suites. *15 rooms | ul. Szpitalna 28 | tel. 012 4 23 23 17 | www. hotelelektor.com.pl*

HOTEL ESTER (114 C3) (*ш F8*)

This hotel is located in the heart of Kazimierz with a view of the old synagogues. The rooms have very tasteful antique-style furniture. *15 rooms | ul. Szeroka 20 | tel. 012 4 26 11 88 | www.hotel-ester.krakow.pl*

HOTEL FLORYAN (110 C2) (*ш E4*)

The rooms in this 16th-century town house are rather modern and not particularly fancy but they are decently equipped and the location is perfect. Hotel guests get a 10 percent reduction on meals in the *Vesuvius Restaurant*. *35 rooms | ul. Floriańska 38 | el. 012 4 311 4 18 | www.floryan.com.pl*

LUXURY HOTELS

Grand Hotel (110 B2) (*ш D4*)

Noblesse oblige: this luxury hotel was opened in the former castle of Princess Marcelina Potocka – a great lover of the arts and one of Frédéric Chopin's pupils – in 1887. The rooms and suites are furnished with antiques; there are tiled stoves in many of the rooms, and the old parquet floors and murals from the period have been preserved. The four restaurants, cafés and bars provide exquisite hospitality. You will even be protected by heavenly powers if you spend the night in Princess Marcelina's private rooms: the magnificent ceiling from the 16th century is painted with small angels. *64 rooms | double rooms from 900 Pln | ul. Sławkowska 5/7 | tel. 012 4 24 08 00 | www.grand.pl*

Hotel Stary ★ �♨ (110 B2) (*ш D4*)

The old town house dates back to the 16th century, although – after several phases of reconstruction – the architectural styles of the 18th and 19th centuries now predominate. The hotel won the 2007 Villegiature Award for the 'best hotel interior design in Europe'. It is a place for those who love history combined with exquisite comfort: the rooms contain dark wooden furniture and silk curtains; exotic woods were used for the parquet flooring, and colourful marble adorns the bathrooms. The hotel also has a small health centre and a terrace café on the roof with a beautiful view. *53 rooms | double rooms from 900 Pln | ul. Szczepańska 5 | tel. 012 3 84 08 08 | www.stary.hotel.com.pl*

Live like a prince in Krakow: the Grand Hotel really lives up to its name

HOTEL MATEJKO (110 C1) (*ᗰ E3*)

Not far away from the railway station in a renovated residential building. Spacious rooms with modern fittings. Good (albeit not particularly quiet) location. *48 rooms | pl. J. Matejki 8 | tel. 01 24 22 47 37 | www.matejkohotel.pl*

HOTEL POD WAWELEM ⁂
(110 A5) (*ᗰ C7*)

Some of the small, modern rooms in this hotel are decorated in rather loud colours. Ask for a room with a balcony and a view of the Vistula. The restaurant and café on the roof have a wonderful view towards the Wawel Castle and over the river. The hotel is only a five-minute walk from the Rynek Główny. *60 rooms | pl. na Groblach 22 | tel. 01 24 26 26 26 | www.hotelpodwawelem.pl*

HOTEL POLESKI ⁂ (113 D3) (*ᗰ C8*)

This modern hotel scores with its high standards. During the summer, there is a restaurant with a unique view of the castle on the roof. The **INSIDER TIP** Classic Panorama rooms with a view of the Vistula and towards the Wawel are especially lovely. *20 rooms | ul. Sandomierska 6 | tel. 01 22 60 54 05 | www.hotelpoleski.pl*

HOTEL POLLERA (110 C2) (*ᗰ E4*)

This magnificent house built in 1834 has now been turned into a hotel, in which you can feel the special atmosphere of times gone by. The **INSIDER TIP** stained-glass windows in the staircase created by Stanisław Wyspiański bring back memories of Art Nouveau days. Thick red and green carpets, comfortable sofas and Tiffany-style lamps make the flair of this exceptional house complete. The suites are exceptionally beautiful. *45 rooms | ul. Szpitalna 30 | tel. 01 24 22 10 44 | www.pollera.com.pl*

HOTEL POLONIA (110 D2) (*ᗰ F4*)

This hotel has a good location but unfortunately the windows of some of the rooms open onto a busy main road. The suites are beautifully appointed; the 19th-century furniture guarantees an authentic period atmosphere. *62 rooms | ul. Basztowa 25 | tel. 01 24 22 12 33 | www. hotel-polonia.com.pl*

den. There are one or two rooms with a shared bathroom on each floor. **INSIDER TIP** Very central but still quiet: the windows of the rooms open onto the neighbouring monastery garden. Breakfast is not served but you can prepare it yourself

Hotel gem in the heart of the old town: Hotel Polski Pod Białym Orłem

HOTEL POLSKI POD BIAŁYM ORŁEM (110 C2) (*ω E4*)

This establishment has been in the possession of the Czartoryski family – a Polish aristocratic family – since 1913. High standard, great location opposite St Florian's Gate, in the heart of the old city in the pedestrian precinct. The suites with their antique-style furnishings are especially beautiful. *54 rooms | ul. Pijarska 17 | tel. 01 24 22 11 44 | www. podorlem. com.pl*

HOTELS: BUDGET

APART HOSTEL (108 C2) (*ω 0*)

Here, the guests live on three floors of a renovated Art Nouveau house with a gar-

in a fully-equipped kitchen. *4 rooms | ul. Siemiradzkiego 15 | tel. 01 26 33 16 15 | www.aparthostel.pl*

HOTEL BONA (117 D4) (*ω 0*)

A good address for people coming by car: quite a distance from the centre but in the heart of the Tyniec Landscape Park. *20 rooms | ul. Tyniecka 167b | tel. 01 22 67 57 73 | www.hotelbona.com.pl*

DOM CASIMI (114 C3) (*ω F8*)

Modern guest rooms in the middle of Kazimierz. Simply equipped, but bright and cheerful. Everything is new and of good quality, and you can also hire bicycles. *12 rooms | ul. Szeroka 7/8 | tel. 01 24 26 11 93 | www.casimi.pl*

APARTAMENTY DELTA (110 C2) *(ᗰ E4)*
Visitors to Krakow can rent holiday flats for 2–10 persons in a town house only five minutes away from the Market Square. Each flat is decorated in a different colour. *4 apts | ul. św. Marka 18 | tel. 01 26 33 21 11 | www.apartamentydelta.pl*

APARTAMENTY MIODOWA
(114 B2) *(ᗰ F7)*
Flats and guest rooms for 1 to 3 persons in the heart of Kazimierz; modern equipment, very sunny, some with a view of ul. Miodowa. Breakfast is served for an extra charge. *3 flats., 3 rooms | ul. Miodowa 21 | tel. 01 24 29 42 07*

NAD RUDAWĄ (117 E4) *(ᗰ 0)*
Family-run bed and breakfast in a private house with a lovely garden and in a quiet area. Lunch and dinner can be provided if desired. *8 rooms | ul. Korbutowej 36 | tel. 01 24 25 36 22 | www.bandb.krakow.com*

OLD CITY APARTMENTS
Though these 30 different apartments are all marketed under the same name, they each have their own style and atmosphere. Located in the centre of Krakow, what they do have in common is modern furnishing and state-of-the-art technology. The apartments in the 'Gothic' series with their unplastered walls will transport you back to the Middle Ages, while the *kiążęcy* ('princely') category offers pure luxury with antique furniture. *Tel. 0606 94 14 83 | www.oldcityapartments.eu*

PENSION TRECIUS ★ (110 C3) *(ᗰ E4)*
Each room in this centrally-located guest house is decorated differently. Stone Gothic columns were discovered in one of the rooms as was a brick wall from the 13th century. The devil himself stayed here once – the impression made by his hoof is evidence of this! There is a 10 per-cent reduction if you book for more than 3 nights. *6 rooms | ul. św. Tomasza 18 | tel. 01 24 24 25 21 | www.trecius.krakow.pl*

PIANO GUESTHOUSE (117 E4) *(ᗰ F1)*
Very centrally located, in the middle of a beautiful garden; breakfast is served on the terrace in summer. Free transfer from the main railway station. Equipped with antique furniture. *6 rooms | ul. Kątowa 4 | tel. 01 26 32 13 71 | www.katowa4.com*

INSIDER TIP **HOTEL ROYAL**
(110 B6) *(ᗰ D7)*
The top address among the budget hotels. Many special offers; call and make enquiries. The biggest plus is its location in the Planty Park at the foot of the Wawel Hill, only 200m from the castle. *120 rooms | ul. św. Gertrudy 26–29 | tel. 01 26 18 40 40 | www.royal.com.pl*

LOW BUDGET

▶ Holders of the ISIC (International Student Identity) card or EURO<26 card are frequently granted reduced prices – not only in hotels but also in museums. *www.euro26online.org, www.isic.org*

▶ You can stay in a room for eight to ten persons in the *Rynek7Hostel* for 50 Pln a night – and that includes a view of the Cloth Hall. An address for young people; there are often parties in the house. Also double rooms. *Rynek Główny 7/6 | tel. 01 24 31 16 98 | www.hostelrynek7.pl*

▶ You can find inexpensive accommodation in Krakow under *www.hostel.pl* and *www.krakow30.com*

WALKING TOURS

The tours are marked in green in the street atlas, the pull-out map and on the back cover

① KLEPARZ – HISTORY OF THE VEGETABLE MARKET DISTRICT

This stroll will take you to Kleparz, a district of Krakow that was an independent city with a large trading centre, town hall and parish church until the 19th century. Visit the church where Pope John Paul II worked as a vicar, meet the crusaders and gorge yourself at the largest fruit and vegetable market in Krakow. The walk takes about 45 minutes.

For many years, Kleparz was allowed to slowly deteriorate; many houses were in a bad state of repair, and restaurants and cafés were non-existent. This district near the train station had a bad reputation as a red-light area, and many people did all they could to avoid it. In the meantime, however, everything has changed for the better. The area around the train station has had a face lift and is now home to the Galeria Krakowska → p. 62, the largest shopping centre in the heart of town. Start out at the northern side of the Barbakane → p. 29. You are now on Plac Matejki (Matejko Square) with the Tannenberg Memorial in the centre. On top of the monument is a figure of the Polish King Władysław Jagiełło proudly riding his horse. It recalls the Battle of

Photo: Vegetable market in Kleparz

A programme full of contrasts, ranging from the Jewish ghetto and vast forests to elegant residential areas and Polish delicacies

Tannenberg that Polish and Lithuanian knights won against the Teutonic Order of Knights in the year 1410. The large marble slab in front of it is dedicated to the Unknown Soldier and is in memory of all the Polish soldiers who fought in the two World Wars. What can be seen today is actually a reconstruction of the original memorial unveiled in 1910, which the Nazis blew up during the Second World War.

You can see the Krakow Art Academy (pl. Matejki 13), a neo-Renaissance building from 1880 on the left side of the street and the Kościół św. Floriana (St Florian's Church) at the other end of the square. It was constructed around the turn of the 12th to 13th century; its present appearance is mainly the result of the Baroque transformation it underwent in the 17th and 18th centuries. The three-nave basilica with two towers and a statue of St Florian has an extremely interesting main altar: it shows a picture of the 17th-century saint extinguishing a fire with the city of Kleparz visible in the background. Karol Wojtyła was vicar and parish priest of this church from 1949 to 1951; this is where the later pope's religious career began. A plaque commemorating John Paul II can be seen hanging on the rectory wall.

Go back to Matejko Square and turn onto ul. Padarewskiego. You will now find your-self standing in front of the **INSIDER TIP** largest *fruit and vegetable market* in the heart of the town *(in summer, daily 9am–6pm, in winter to 4pm | pl. Kleparski)*. Here, you can find everything you need: fruit and vegetables, cheese, ham and bread. Peasant women, who sometimes travel up to 100km (62mi) to come to the market, sell their specialities (such as cheese from Zakopane) on wooden tables at the far right end of the square. There is also a large flower market here.

2 ZWIERZYNIEC – IN THE KINGS' GARDEN

This walk takes you past churches and monasteries to the centre of a picturesque residential district. You leave the centre of Krakow and come out into the countryside where you will be able to enjoy a fabulous view of the entire town. This excursion also makes a fine bicycle tour that you can extend to include a small additional excursion to the Wolski Forest. Without the detour, the walk should normally take about 1.5 hours.

You start at the foot of Wawel Hill by the Vistula and walk in the direction of ul. Kościuszki. If you decide to hire a bicycle, ride along the bank of the Vistula. The district of Zwierzyniec (Zoo) includes the former hunting grounds and gardens of the Polish Kings and the estates of the Klasztor Norbertanek (Convent of the

Unusual, but all the more impressive for that reason: the wooden Church of St Margaret

Premonstratensian Nuns) that you will reach after around 10 minutes. Nuns still live in the convent and therefore this building is not open to the public. However, it is well worth visiting the Baroque Church of St Augustine and John the Baptist *(daily ul. Kościuski 88)* that is part of the complex: the history of the largest nunnery in the country dates back to the 12th century. This single-nave church was created around 500 years later when the house of worship was enlarged and adapted to the Baroque style. This is where the nuns sat during mass because they were forbidden to have any contact to the outside world and 'normal believers'.

After you visit the church, turn left and cross the road. The route past Aleja Waszyngtona goes uphill and through the most exclusive residential area in Krakow. On the left, you will see a rare example of sacred wooden architecture *(ul. św. Bronisłay 3)* the Kościół św. Małgorzaty (St Margaret's Church) from the 17th century; unfortunately, it can only be visited from outside. It is an octagonal construction and was used as a place of worship for plague victims.

Zwierzyniec is now a district of Krakow but has preserved its suburban character in many areas. It is dominated by architecture from the 19th and early 20th centuries nestled in spacious parkland areas. Most of the housing in this area originated during the period when it was popular to build multi-family houses in green areas on the outskirts of large towns. The ul. Gontyny is an especially picturesque street.

If you continue along the Aleja Waszyngtona, you will see one of the oldest churches in the city on the right-hand side; it is the Kościół Najśw. Salwatora (Church of the Redeemer) *(only during masses on Sunday | ul św Bronisławy 9)*. The single-nave stone Romanesque church was built

in the 12th century and has retained most of its original character.

As you walk further along the chestnut-lined avenue to the Kościuszko Mound → p. 22, you will pass the Salwator Cemetery, with its interesting graves from the 19th century, on the left. The mound was raised in the years between 1820 and 1823 as a memorial to the freedom fighter Kościuszko. One can still see the remains of the red-brick fortress that the Austrians later built around it. Climb up the 34m (111ft)-high hillock to feast your eyes on a unique view over the city *(daily 9am until twilight | entrance fee 6 Pln)* and afterwards reward yourself with a cup of coffee in the *Kawiarnia pod Kopcem (Aleja Waszyngtona | tel. 01 26 62 20 29)* in the restored section of the fortification complex.

If you still feel like it and have enough stamina, keep on walking or peddling towards Las Wolki (Wolki Forest). This is Krakow's green lung and, with an area of 1075 acres, the largest forest park in Poland. There you will discover more than 40km (25mi) of footpaths and cycle trails, the Ogród Zoologiczny (zoological Gardens) → p. 88 and the Klasztor Kamedułów (Cloister of the Camaldolese Hermits) *(daily 8–11am and 3–4pm for 15 minutes, only for men – women allowed during religious festivals)*. Catch bus 134 from the zoo back to the centre of town; you can take your cycle with you.

3 HISTORY AND MODERN ART

This walk takes you to the southern side of the Vistula through the suburb of Podgórze. This formerly independent city, which received its rights and privileges from Emperor Josef II in 1784, has been a suburb of Krakow since 1915 and is now enjoying a real boom period. New restaurants and cafés, galleries and museums, are being opened everywhere and paths for cyclists and pedestrians established. You will be able to have a cup of coffee with a view of the Vistula, admire modern Polish and international art, and take a break in the Bednarski Park on this tour, which you can also do on a bike. The confrontation with the ghetto where the German occupiers confined the Krakow's Jewish citizens from 1941 to 1943 is a harrowing experience. The walk will take about 2.5 hours.

You start the tour on the right bank of the Vistula at Plac Wolnica in Kazimierz; the best way to reach it is by tram (lines 6 and 8) – that is if you are not taking the bike *(cycle hire in Kazimierz, see Travel Tips)*. After you get off, walk on down Krakowska Street towards the Vistula. Before you cross the river, turn to the left and you will be able to see the remains of Krakow's infancy on the left in the form of the ancient medieval city walls. On the new pedestrian bridge over the Vistula,

the kładka Bernatka, devoted couples have hung countless padlocks on the railing in the hope that their love will last forever.

This romantic gesture leads you into Podgórze: you will see a small green area with a few restaurants around it in front of you – they include the cult pub Drukarnia *(ul. Nadwiślańska 1 | www.drukarnia-podgorze. pl)* in a Classicist house from around the turn of the 19th century and the Cava Restaurant *(ul. Nadwiślańska 1 | tel. 01 26 56 74 56 | www.cafecava.pl)* that specialises in snails. If they are not your favourite food, the Pod Lwem *(Mon–Sat 8am– 10pm, Sun 9am–10pm | ul. Józefińska 4 | tel. 01 25 19 37 47 37)* is an ideal alternative restaurant for a light lunch. Continue straight ahead along the Staromostowa until you see the Market Square of the former city of Podgórze in front of you. The old and new town halls, as well as the largest church in the district, the Kościół św. Józefa *(St Josef's Church: ul. Zamojskiego 2 | jozef.diecezja.pl)*, are located on the Rynek Podgórski. The combination

You can tell that Kazimierz was once an independent city: urban flair on the Plac Wolnica

Memories of unbearable life in the ghetto in the Pharmacy under the Eagle

of red bricks with bright-coloured, local sandstone and limestone is a special characteristic of this neo-Gothic house of worship that was built between 1905 and 1909. The Park Bednarskiego, a 30 acre-green oasis that was laid out at the end of the 19th century, starts behind the church and is the perfect place to take a short rest. After that, it is back to the Rynek Podgórski, past the square and to the right onto ul. Limanowskiego. The neo-Classicist building on the corner (constructed in the years 1844–1854) is the former New Town Hall (ul. Rynek Podgórski 1) and now the home of the district administration. On ul. Limanowskiego, you are already in the area of the former ghetto where the Jewish population of Krakow was interned from March 1941 to March 1943. Make a short detour to ul. Węgierska to the former Synagogue (Synagoga Zuckera) that was built in 1880 and destroyed during the Second World War. A private person bought the ruins in the 1990s and this is now the site of the Gallery Starmach (Mon–Fri 11am–6pm | ul. Węgierska | www.starmach.com.pl), which exhibits modern Polish art.

Back on ul. Limanowskiego, turn left onto ul. Na Zjeździe at the next traffic light and you will reach the Plac Bohaterów Getta (Ghetto Heroes Square) → p. 49. The deeply moving history of the ghetto and the chemist Tadeusz Pankiewicz, who saved many Jews from being murdered by the Nazis, is recounted in the Museum Apteka Pod Orłem (Pharmacy under the Eagle) → p. 49. As you continue your tour, you will discover original remains of the ghetto walls in the form of *macevas* (Jewish gravestones) on ul. Lwowska. Carry on towards the train tracks and pass under them on Tadeuscza Romaowcza before turning left onto ul. Lipowa. You will now see the building of the former Schindler Factory → p. 46 in front of you. This is where the City Museum displays an impressive exhibition on 'Krakow under Nazi Occupation 1939–1945'. Krakow's MOCAK (Museum of Modern Art) → p. 47, which organises fascinating exhibitions of works by Polish and international artists, is also located on the grounds of the former Deutsche Emailwarenfabrik (German Enamelware Factory) (D.E.F.)

TRAVEL WITH KIDS

The Poles love children and are fairly tolerant. In recent years, there has been a real boom in the number of births – and you can see children and prams on every corner. However, baby's changing tables, high chairs and play areas are still rare in restaurants – except for those in large shopping centres. The activities available for (foreign) children are also rather limited in Krakow. It is up to the parents once again: they will have to show their offspring just how fascinating the Old Town, the dragon's cave and majestic castle really are.

AKWARIUM I MUZEUM PRZYRODNICZE PAN (AQUARIUM & MUSEUM OF NATURAL HISTORY) ●
(110 C5) *(𝒲 E7)*
Nowhere else in Poland can you find so many tropical fish, amphibians and reptiles in one place. You will also be dazzled by all the colourful fish and luminescent creatures from the depths of the ocean. A pair of small cotton top tamarin monkeys adds another exotic touch to these surroundings – not only because they come from the rainforests of Colombia. *Mon–Fri 9am–8pm, Sat/Sun 9am–9pm | entrance fee children 14 Pln, adults 20 Pln | ul. św. Sebastiana 9 | 10 min walk from the Market Square| www.aquariumkrakow.com*

AQUAPARK (117 E4) *(𝒲 0)*
The swimming pools and ponds in the largest complex of this kind in Poland cover an area of 0.5 acres; the main attraction is a 200m-long water slide. Parents will also find plenty to do: yoga and tai-chi courses are offered in the health centre, and they can tone up their bodies in the fitness rooms. The complex also has a restaurant, a café and several small shops. *Daily 8am–10pm | entrance fee per hour: children 15 Pln, adults 19 Pln (with sauna 26 Pln), happy hour 8–9am: children 9 Pln, adults 12 Pln | ul. Dobrego Pasterza 126 | www.parkwodny.pl*

OGRÓD ZOOLOGICZNY (ZOOLOGICAL GARDENS) (117 D4) *(𝒲 0)*
Built on the site of a former pheasant breeding farm in 1927, this is one of the oldest zoos in the country. More than 1500 animals, including 32 species threatened with extinction, live on the 49 acres of land. Younger members of the family will

Where the wild dragons live: a little bit of imagination is all that is needed, and then the youngsters will love Krakow, too

be particularly fascinated by the mini-zoo where guinea pigs, rabbits, ponies and small pot-bellied pigs wait to be petted and fed *(you can buy food at the zoo)*. The zoo's beautiful location in the Wolski Forest makes it well worth a visit; especially in May when the azaleas and rhododendrons are in full bloom.

During the week, you can drive to the gates of the zoo *(parking fee 6 Pln)*, but you have to leave your car about half a mile away from the zoo at the weekend and then walk the rest of the way or take the shuttle bus. *Daily 9am–7pm | entrance fee children 10 Pln, adults 18 Pln | Aleja Kasy Oszczędności Miasta Krakowa 14 | www.zoo-krakow. pl | bus 134: Hotel Cracovia*

INSIDER TIP ▶ PARK JORDANA
(108 A6) *(ϻ A6)*

This 49-acre park has footpaths, children's playgrounds, football and volleyball grounds, as well as a small lake where the youngsters can have fun in pedal boats. The park, which was opened in 1889, is one of Poland's oldest and specifically conceived as a place for children and adolescents to play and do sport. The largest meadow in the city, the *Błonia*, is on the other side of the road and offers another great place for children to romp around. *Daily 9 am to dusk | entrance free | Aleja 3 Maja | tram 15, 18: Park Jordana*

TEATR GROTESKA (108 B–C4) *(ϻ B4)*
The small theatre produces famous Polish and international fairytales for children; also as puppet shows. Although the performances are only in Polish, children who don't speak the language will still be captivated. The theatre also organises Krakow's annual dragon parades. *Performances daily | ul. Skarbowa 2 | tel. 0126 33 48 22 | www.groteska.pl*

FESTIVALS & EVENTS

People in Krakow like to celebrate and do so whenever they can – usually on the Rynek Główny, but during the City Festival in June all of Krakow becomes a gigantic stage. There are many other open-air festivals in the calendar, along with concerts and processions through the streets. Information under *www.biurofestiwalowe.pl* or from the tourist information office.

PUBLIC HOLIDAYS

1 Jan *(New Year's Day)*; **Easter Monday; 1 May** *(Labour Day)*; **3 May** *(Constitution Day)*; **Corpus Christi; 15 Aug** *(Assumption)*; **1 Nov** *(All Saints' Day)*; **11 Nov** *(Independence Day)*; **25/26 Dec** *(Christmas)*

EVENTS

MARCH

The ▶ *Dni Bachowskie (Bach Days)* at the end of the month are organised by the Krakow Music Academy. Throughout the week, there are lectures and performances of Baroque music (not only by Bach) played by Krakow students and other musicians. *www.amuz.krakow.pl*

APRIL

The one week ▶ *Misteria Paschalia* festival features classical concerts in churches, the Philharmonic Hall and the opera house. Theme: Lent and Easter. *www.misteria paschalia.pl*. Jazz fans should not miss out on the international ▶ *Starzy i Mlodzi czyli Jazz w Krakowie (Old and New – Jazz in Krakow)* festival. Famous and less well-known musicians give concerts in jazz cellars, clubs and cafés. *www.jazz.krakow.pl*

MAY

You will be able to visit most of the collections almost free of charge on the ▶ *Noc Muzeów w Krakowie (Long Night of the Museums)*. A specially-minted 1 Pln coin is your entrance ticket. This event is extremely popular and you should thus expect long queues at the various museums.

JUNE

Concerts, parades, marathon runs and other events are all part of the ▶ *Święto Miasta (City Festival)* at the beginning of June. The spectacular highlight is the ▶ ● *Parada Smoków (Dragon Parade)* when those taking part pull gigantic colourful

Krakow bubbles with joie-de-vivre, and it is not only during the Festival of Jewish Culture that it enjoys exuberant celebrations

dragon figures through Krakow's streets. The ▶ *Wianki (Vistula Wreath Festival)* on midsummer night brings back memories of pagan days when young girls cast wreaths into the water on the longest night of the year in the hope that fate would send them a loving husband. Also on the programme: Concerts with top international stars like Lenny Kravitz and Jamiroquai, and a fireworks display.

Kazimierz celebrates the ▶ ★ *Festiwal Kultury Żydowskiej (Festival of Jewish Culture)* with concerts, films and exhibitions. The guided tours to places that are closed at other times are fascinating. *www.jewish festival.pl*

AUGUST

The ▶ *Targi Sztuki Ludowej (Folk Art Markets)* focuses on the arts and crafts of Krakow. Traditional products made of wood and clay are sold on the Rynek Główny.

SEPTEMBER

The ▶ INSIDER TIP *Festiwal Sacrum Profanum* is a week-long music festival held in original locations: in the former Schindler Factory for example, or a rolling mill in Nowa Huta. The focus is on all genres of 20th-century music from Polish jazz and the Ensemble Modern to Kraftwerk, the pioneers of electronic music. Classical music, ballet and jazz are performed in the Philharmonic Hall. *www.sacrumprofanum.pl*

DECEMBER

The ▶ *Targi Bożonarodzeniowe (Christmas Market)* takes over the Market Square. The most beautiful nativity cribs are chosen during the ▶ INSIDER TIP *Konkurs Szopek Krakowskich (Crib Festival)* on the Market Square and then exhibited in the Historical Museum. *Muzeum Historyczne Masta Krakowa: entrance fee 3 Pln | Rynek Główny 35 | mhk.pl*

LINKS, BLOGS, APPS & MORE

LINKS

▶ en.karnet.krakow.pl Internet magazine dealing with all kinds of Krakow cultural subjects from music, literature, theatre and exhibitions to cinema and the various festivals

▶ http://en.poland.gov.pl This official promotional website provides loads of useful and interesting information about Poland in general. The site is well structured and topics range from history, geography and culture to science, business and politics

▶ www.guardian.co.uk/travel/krakow England's well-known daily has a special page dedicated to Krakow; it is regularly updated

▶ krakow4u.pl/eng_index.php?parametr=eng_glowna_s Dozens of fabulous photos of Krakow; 360° shots of sights such as the Franciscan Church are particularly impressive

▶ www.wawel.net Countless photos of Krakow taken by a professional photographer

▶ www.allaboutjazz.com For all who did not know that Krakow was a jazz centre – an introduction to Polish jazz: 'Polish jazz for dummies: 60 years of jazz from Poland'

BLOGS & FORUMS

▶ www.urbantravelblog.com/guide/krakow This blog by professional travel writers has a nicely written article about Krakow, which also manages to communicate the spirit of the city and the people.

▶ www.cracow-life.com As the name suggest, a forum with a lively, well-informed English-language guide, covering all aspects of life in Krakow

▶ krakowski.blox.pl/html The 'Krakow Day by Day' photo-blog is unfortunately only in Polish but the great pictures speak for themselves

Regardless of whether you are still preparing your trip or already in Krakow: these addresses will provide you with more information, videos and networks to make your holiday even more enjoyable

▶ www.krak.tv The film reports from Krakow on various topics; it is in Polish but still provides an interesting insight into everyday life

▶ www.youtube.com youtube has a variety of cultural and historical clips about Krakow; it is certainly worth browsing through the selection. The quality is very mixed

▶ www.polishpod101.com & bloggy-polish.co.uk Two 'slightly' different approaches to learning Polish with podcasts!

▶ de.worldcam.eu/index.php?s=szukaj&szukany=Krakow Collection of webcams scattered throughout the city with views of the Wawel, Rynek Główny, the University and other places

▶ www.youtube.com/watch?v=Xmg-7R72caQ&feature=related You can experience the trumpeter in St Mary's Church playing the *hejnał* live in this short film

▶ www.youtube.com/watch?v=Cr4YE_hh4HI The finale of the Krakow Festival of Jewish Culture is a uniquely exhilarating klezmer concert

▶ Krakow in my pocket Useful app when working out how to get from A to B

▶ Around me This app for your iPhone and Android searches the neighbourhood and provides a list of hotels, cash dispensers, restaurants, pubs, etc

▶ www.spottedbylocals.com/krakow What do the locals recommend when they receive guests in their home town?

▶ www.couchsurfing.org Krakow also has a lot of followers in the worldwide network of couchsurfers. Around 3500 Krakow inhabitants offer travellers their couch, their hospitality and their local knowledge

TRAVEL TIPS

ARRIVAL

✈ All national and international flights land at the *Kraków Airport (www.krakowairport.pl)*. There are regular services from the UK operated by the Polish airline LOT *(www.lot.com)*, British Airways *(www.britishairways.com)* EasyJet *(www.easyjet.com)* Ryanair *(www.ryanair.com)*, Lufthansa *(www.lufthansa.com)*, and Austrian Airlines *(www.austrian.com)*. You can take bus 292 or 208 from the airport, both travel to the main train station (2.60 Pln), or the train that takes you there directly. There is a shuttle bus from the airport (200m away) to the station; the ticket costs 8 Pln. The train departs every 30 minutes and the trip to the main station takes 16 minutes. A taxi to the centre of Krakow costs around 55 Pln.

�car It is about 1430km (890mi) from London to Krakow in a straight line (which would be straight across Belgium, Germany and south-east from Wrocław). Not to be recommended for a weekend trip!

🚆 The train is no problem. Take the lunchtime Eurostart to Brussels, the high-speed train to Cologne and then the overnight sleeper train 'Jan Kiepura' from Cologne to Warsaw. There are direct connections from Warsaw to Krakow. Alternatively, take the Eurostar to Paris and then the City Night Line sleeper from Paris to Berlin and an express train to Warsaw. Travelling across Europe is great fun. For train information, see *www.seat61.com*

BANKS & EXCHANGE

There are not only branches of all major banks in Krakow *(in general: Mon–Fri 7.30am–5pm, Sat 7.30am–2pm)* but also privately operated exchange offices: *kantor (daily 9am–7pm)*. However, it is much less complicated to take money from one of the many cash dispensers in the city using your EC or credit card.

CONSULATES & EMBASSIES

BRITISH EMBASSY
Ul. Kawalerii 12 | 00-468 Warsaw | tel. +48 22 311 00 00 | ukinpoland.fco.gov.uk/en/

U.S. CONSULATE GENERAL
Ul. Stolarska 9 | 31-043 Krakow | tel. +48 124 24 51 00 | poland.usembassy.gov

CANADIAN EMBASSY
Ul. Jana Matejki 1/5 | 00-481 Warsaw | +48 22 584 31 00 | www.canadainternational.gc.ca/poland-pologne

RESPONSIBLE TRAVEL

It doesn't take a lot to be environmentally friendly whilst travelling. Don't just think about your carbon footprint whilst flying to and from your holiday destination but also about how you can protect nature and culture abroad. As a tourist it is especially important to respect nature, look out for local products, cycle instead of driving, save water and much more. If you would like to find out more about eco-tourism please visit: *www.ecotourism.org*

From arrival to weather

Holiday from start to finish: the most important addresses and information for your Krakow trip

CURRENCY

Poland's national currency is the *złoty (1 złoty = 100 groszy)*. It is sometimes possible to pay in euros; only notes are accepted and the change is given in *złoty*.

CUSTOMS

Goods for personal consumption can be imported and exported tax-free in the EU including 800 cigarettes, 10 litres of spirits, 90 litres of wine and 110 litres of beer. It is necessary to get authorisation from the Polish Ministry of Culture if you wish to export any antiques made before 9 May 1945.

Travellers to the United States who are returning residents of the country do not have to pay duty on articles purchased overseas up to the value of $800, but there are limits on the amount of alcoholic beverages and tobacco products. For the regulations for international travel for U.S. residents please see *www.cbp.gov*

CYCLING

All in all, there are only around 30km (19mi) of marked cycle lanes in Krakow. The loveliest and safest places to ride are along the Vistula (to Tyniec or Nowa Huta), in Błonia, the Planty and in Las Wolski (Wolski Forest). You can hire a bike for an average price of 30 to 35 Pln/day. Cycle hire: the most central is *Rent a bike (May–Oct daily 9am to dusk | ul. św. Anny 4)* (110 B3) *(ɰ D5)*, in Kazimierz Dwa koła *(May–Oct daily 9am–7pm | ul. Józefa 5)* (114 B4) *(ɰ E8)*; Art-Bike *(daily 30–50 Pln, or 5 Pln/hour. | ul. Starowiślna 33a)* (114 B1) *(ɰ F7)*.

BUDGETING

Beer	from £2/$3.10 for 0.5 litres in a restaurant
Cappuccino	from £1.60/$2.50 for a cup in a café
Pizza	from £5/$8 in a restaurant
Cinema	from £3/$4.70 for a ticket
Museum	from £1/$1.60 per person
Bus	from £0.50/$0.70 for one trip

DRIVING

The speed limit on motorways is 140kph (85mph); in built-up areas (white signs) and within towns (green signs) 50kph – 60kph (30mph – 35mph) from 11pm to 6am. There are frequent speed checks! Dipped beams are obligatory during the day and there must be a reflective vest in the boot.

If you do decide to drive to Krakow, you will soon discover that parking in the city is anything but easy. The inner city is divided into three parking zones: Zone A (centre) is reserved for pedestrians. You are only allowed to drive to your hotel to unload your luggage; parking is strictly prohibited. There is a speed limit of 20kph in Zone B and you are only permitted to park at a limited number of marked spaces. Parking is permitted in Zone C after you have paid the appropriate fee: 3 Pln for the first hour on weekdays between 10am and 6pm (free on week-ends). You can buy parking tickets at post offices, from street vendors and from machines (only cash; the machines do not give change). The minimum fee is 1 Pln/ 20 min.

ELECTRICITY

220 volt alternating current with the (type C & E) Europlug.

EMERGENCY SERVICES

Police *tel. 997*; fire brigade *tel. 998*, ambulance *tel. 999*

IMMIGRATION

Citizens of the U.K. & Ireland, U.S., Canada, Australia and New Zealand need only a valid passport to enter all countries of the EU. Children below the age of 12 need a children's passport.

INFORMATION ABROAD

POLISH NATIONAL TOURIST OFFICE
Level 3, Westgate House | West Gate | London W5 1YY | tel. +44 030 03 03 18 12 | www.poland.travel/en-gb
5 Marine View Plaza, Suite 303b | Hoboken, NJ 07030-5722 | tel. +12 01 420-99 10 | www.poland.travel/en-us

INFORMATION IN KRAKOW

There are many city information offices *(informacja)*, as well as private information spots, in the centre of Krakow. You can book tours and excursions to Zakopane, Wieliczka, Auschwitz and other destinations, and buy concert tickets from most of them. The *Karnet Magazin*, a brochure listing all the current events in Polish and English that is published monthly, is available at *ul. Jana 2* (110 B3) *(𝄞 D4)*. Additional information offices: *Wieża Ratuszowa,*

BOOKS & FILMS

▶ **Unseen Hand** – Adam Zagajewski, one of the world's master poets has written a brilliant new collection of prose in which he returns to themes that have played an important role in his career – meditations on language, place, and history (2011)

▶ **The Girl in the Red Coat** – As a child, Roma Ligocka survived the Holocaust in the Krakow ghetto (2003)

▶ **Pope John Paul II** – John Kent Harrison's film is a moving depiction of the man whose courage and convictions were to make him the most popular pope of the 20th century (2005)

▶ **Schindler's List** – Shot in Krakow, Steven Spielberg's film recounts the story of the 1100 Jews saved by Oskar Schindler (1993)

▶ **The Cracow Ghetto Pharmacy** – Tadeusz Pankiewicz was the only non-Jew allowed to stay in the Krakow ghetto and run the pharmacy. His memoir reports on the horrific cruelty that he witnessed while he was there (1982)

▶ **The Pianist** – Roman Polanski's film is based on the true story of the gifted pianist Władysław Szpilman who spent five years struggling to stay alive in Nazi-occupied Poland (2002)

Rynek główny 1 (Town Hall Tower) (110 B3) (ℳ D5); *Małopolskie Centrum Informacji Turystycznej, Rynek Główny 1/3 (Cloth Hall)* (110 B3) (ℳ D5) | *www.mcit.pl*

INTERNET

The official site of the city with an up-to-date calendar of events is *www.krakow.pl.* The comprehensive *www.Krakowonline. com* provides all of the necessary information for your stay. You will find interesting hotels under *www.krakow-hotel-guide.com* and apartments at *www.krakow-apart ments.com*.

INTERNET CAFÉS & WI-FI

There are two Wi-Fi zones in Krakow: on the Market Square *(net name: Krakow123)* and on ul Szeroka in Kazimierz; but both only provide a very sluggish connection. Many cafés and most restaurants provide somewhat faster Internet access.

A password, which you will be given free of charge by the waiter or waitress (for a limited period), is usually necessary. There are also many Internet cafés in the city. One hour of surfing costs 2–4 Pln. In the centre: *Cornet (ul. Gołębia 4)* (110 B3–4) (ℳ D5), *Planet (Rynek Główny 24)* (110 B3) (ℳ D5), *Klub internetowy Szewska (ul. Szewska 21)* (110 B3) (ℳ D4), *Internetcafé Bracka (ul. Bracka 3–5)* (110 B3) (ℳ D5).

MEDICAL SERVICES

The same conditions apply as for all other EU countries. The European Insurance Card guarantees treatment for those legally insured; the costs are refunded in keeping with the rates in your home country (don't forget the bills!). Travel insurance is necessary for any additional services.

NEWSPAPERS

You can buy international daily papers and magazines in some hotels or from the *Empik* bookshop on the Market Square *(daily 9am–10pm | Rynek Główny 5)*.

OPENING HOURS

There are no restrictions on opening hours in Poland and most shops do business from 10am to 6pm on weekdays and usually to 3pm at the weekend. However, there are food shops in the centre of town that stay open until 10pm or even around the clock. The large shopping centres and chain stores are open to 10pm during the week and 8pm on Saturday and Sunday.

PERSONAL SAFETY

Krakow is one of the safest towns in Poland; normal precautions are sufficient. There are usually no problems in the inner city at night but you should avoid districts such as Nova Huta and Podgórze when it is dark.

PHONES & MOBILE PHONES

Dialling code for Australia: *0061*, Canada: *001*, Ireland: *00353*, UK: *0044*, USA: *001* Dialling code for Poland: *0048*, followed by the code for Krakow *12* and the telephone number. You also have to dial the city code without *0: 12* if you call within Krakow (or from other parts of Poland).

Most public telephones only accept cards; they can be bought from the post offices and at tobacconists. The most inexpensive solution if you have a telephone without a SIM lock is to buy a Polish prepaid SIM card *(karta sim*, at post offices, in the *trafik*, and some bookshops). If you do buy a Polish SIM card and want to call a fixed-line number, you dial *012* and then the number or just the mobile phone number. The code from a British mobile phone is *004812*.

CURRENCY CONVERTER

£	PLN	PLN	£
1	5.20	1	0.20
3	15.50	3	0.60
5	26	5	1
13	67	13	2.50
40	207	40	7.70
75	388	75	14.50
120	620	120	23
250	1295	250	48
500	2590	500	97

$	PLN	PLN	$
1	3.30	1	0.30
3	10	3	0.90
5	16.50	5	1.50
13	43	13	4
40	132	40	12
75	247	75	23
120	395	120	36
250	825	250	75
500	1650	500	150

For current exchange rates see www.xe.com

POST

You can purchase stamps and envelopes from the post office (poczta). The most central ones are the *post office on Plac Wszystkich Świętych 9 (Mon–Fri 8am–6pm)* (110 B4) *(𝕄 D5)* and the *main post office (Mon–Fri 7.30am–8.30pm, Sat 8am–2pm | ul. Westerplatte 20)* (110 C4) *(𝕄 E5)*, the *post office at ul. Lubicz 4* (111 D2) *(𝕄 E–F 3–4) (near the train station)* is open 24 hours a day. Postcards and letters up to 100g: 3 Pln to all European destinations.

PUBLIC TRANSPORT

The fastest and cheapest way to get around in Krakow is by bus or tram; most run until around 11pm. A ticket *(billet auto-busowy)* costs 2.50 Pln (3 Pln from the conductor). You can buy tickets from machines and some *trafik*, kiosks that sell newspapers, cigarettes and drinks. There are two ticket booths in the centre: *ul. Podwale 3/5* (110 A3) *(𝕄 C4)* and *ul. Mogilska 15a* (117 E4) *(𝕄 J3) (both Mon–Fri 7am–7pm)*. A ticket is valid for one journey; you have to cancel another one if you change. In this such cases, it is better to buy a one-hour ticket that includes changes *(3.10 Pln)*. Also available: 24, 48 and 72-hour tickets *(10.40 Pln, 18.80 Pln and 25 Pln)* or a week's pass *(38 Pln)*.

SIGHTSEEING TOURS & GUIDED TOURS

The meeting place for *city walks* is on Plac Mariacki 3 (110 C3) *(𝕄 E5)* (you can also get maps there). Tours in English are organised by KrakowTours *7 S | c | epanski Square | tel. 012 4113609 | www.krakow-tours.pl.* There are separate tours: 9am–1pm through the inner city, and Kazimierz in the afternoon. *50 Pln/person | tel. 01 24 31 16 78.* Also free walking tours through the inner city; meeting place St Mary's Church, 11am.

On another tour, you will be able to admire the city from a double-decker bus *(start: Wawel at the Hotel Royal)*. The bus stops at several places and the ticket is valid for the entire day. *36 Pln/person | tickets pl. Mariacki 3.*

Die *Communist Tour* presents a panorama of the history of the individual districts of Krakow in the years from 1945 to 1989 *(2.5 hours 130 Pln/person);* the most popular tour *(4 hours)* including lunch, a glass of vodka, the screening of a propaganda film and a visit to a flat decorated in the style of those times, costs 170 Pln per person. *www.crazyguides.pl*

Horse-drawn coaches for 4–5 guests stop at the main Market Square and on ul. Kanonicza *(30 min Market Square to Wawel | 150 Pln)*. Officially, only licensed guides are allowed to give *city tours* of Krakow. *www.insiders.pl* organises tours devoted to unusual subjects.

From April to October, you will be able to discover the city from the river on board the 'Nimfa' a ship used for ● *Vistula tours*. The cruises start from 10am to 5.30pm from Monday to Saturday and at 10am, 1 and 4.30pm on Sunday and cost 15 Pln. The last trip on Sunday is combined with a visit to the Benedictine abbey in Tyniec: While the ship casts off immediately at other times, on this trip you will have an hour's time to visit the abbey before travelling back with the 'Nimfa' *(minimum 20 passengers | 35 Pln). Bulwar Czerwieński 3, dock Przystań Wawel, in front of the Grunwaldzki Bridge* (113 D4) *(ᗰ C8)* | *tel. 0530 75 07 36 | www.statek krakow.com*

TAXIS

Taxis are relatively inexpensive. There are several taxi ranks in the centre, and elsewhere you can use your mobile phone to call one. Normally, the taximeter is turned on: it usually shows 5 Pln when you get in and then there is a kilometre charge starting at 3 Pln depending on the tariff (weekday, holiday, day/night rate).

TIPPING

Tips are not included and it is customary to round up the bill. In higher-class restaurants, 10 percent is usual.

WEATHER IN KRAKOW

	Jan	Feb	March	April	May	June	July	Aug	Sept	Oct	Nov	Dec
Daytime temperatures in °C/°F												
	–1/30	2/36	7/45	14/57	19/66	22/72	24/75	24/75	20/68	13/55	7/45	2/36
Nighttime temperatures in °C/°F												
	–6/21	–5/23	–1/30	4/39	9/48	12/54	15/59	14/57	10/50	5/41	1/34	–3/27
Sunshine hours/day												
	1	2	3	5	6	7	7	6	5	3	2	1
Precipitation days/month												
	8	7	8	8	11	12	10	9	8	8	9	10

USEFUL PHRASES POLISH

PRONUNCIATION

In Polish, sentences are often formed depending on the gender of the speaker or the person being addressed. That is why, in some cases, there are two versions in this list of phrases: the first is masculine; the second, feminine.

IN BRIEF

Yes/No/Maybe	tak [tuk]/nie [nyay]/może [moshay]
Please/Thank you	Proszę [Proshen]/Dziękuję [Djenkooyay]
Excuse me, please	Przepraszam! [Psheprashamm]
May I ...?	Czy mogę ...? [Tschi moshay ...?]
Pardon?	Słucham? [Suukamm?]
I would like to .../	Chciałbym/Chciałabym ... [Chowbim/-chowabim ...]/
Have you got ...?	Czy ma pan/pani ...? [Chi ma pan/pani ...?]
How much is ...	Ile to kosztuje ...? [Iletta kostooya ...?]
I (don't) like that	To mi się (nie) podoba [To mi shen (nyay) podobba]
good/bad	dobrze/źle [dobshey/shlay]
broken/doesn't work	rozbity/nie działa [rosbyeti/nyay tsiaua]
too much/much/little	za dużo/dużo/mało [za dusho/duscho/maavo]
all/nothing	wszystko/nic [shistko/neets]
Help!/Attention!/	Ratunku!/Uwaga!/Ostrożnie!
Caution!	[Ratunnku!/Uvaga!/Ostroshniyeh!]
ambulance	karetka pogotowia [karetka pogotoviya]
police/fire brigade	policja/straż pożarna [policia/strash posharna]
danger/dangerous	niebezpieczeństwo/niebezpieczny [nyebyestpetshtvo/nyebyestpetshnya]

GREETINGS, FAREWELL

Good morning!/afternoon!	Dzień dobry! [jen dobry!]
Good evening!/night!	Dobry wieczór!/Dobranoc! [Dobbri vechor!/Dobbranots!]
Hello!/Goodbye!	Witam!/Do widzenia! [Vitam!/Do vidseniya!]
See you!	Cześć! [Chesh!]
My name is ...	Nazywam się ... [Nasivam shen ...]
What's your name?	Jak się nazywasz? [Yak shen nasivash?]
I'm from ...	Pochodzę z ... [Pokodsen s ...]

Czy mówisz po polsku?

"Do you speak Polish?" This guide will help you to say the basic words and phrases in Polish

DATE & TIME

Monday/Tuesday	poniedziałek/wtorek [ponyedsyavek/vstorrek]
Wednesday/Thursday	środa/czwartek [srodda/chvartekk]
Friday/Saturday	piątek/sobota [piyontekk/sobotta]
Sunday	niedziela [nyedsyella]
working day	dzień roboczy [jen robottchi]
holiday	dzień świąteczny [jen sviyontetshni]
today/tomorrow/	dziś/jutro [dyish/yutro]/
yesterday	wczoraj [vchorai]
hour/minute	godzina/minuta [godsina/minuta]
day/night/week	dzień/noc/tydzień [jen/notts/tidshinya]
What time is it?	Która godzina? [Ktura godsina?]

TRAVEL

open/closed	otwarte/zamknięte [otvarteh/samkniyente]
entrance/vehicle entrance	wejście/wyjście [veyshyeh/veeshyeh]
departure/arrival	odjazd/przyjazd [odyast/pshiyast]
toilets – ladies/	toaleta damska [toaletta damska]/
toilets – gentlemen	toaleta męska [myanska]
(no) drinking water	Woda nie zdatna do picia/Woda pitna [Voda statna do pidya/Voda pitna]
Where is ...?/	Gdzie jest ...? [Gsay yest...?]
Where are ...?	Gdzie są ...? [Gsay song ...?]
left/right	na lewo/na prawo [na levo/na prahvo]
straight ahead/back	prosto/spowrotem [prosto/spavrottem]
close/far	blisko/daleko [blisko/dalehko]
bus/tram	autobus/tramwaj [autobus/tramveye]
metro/taxi	metro/taxi [metro/taxi]
street map/map	mapa miasta/mapa [mapa myasta/mapa]
train station	dworzec/lotnisko [dvashek/lotnissko]
schedule/ticket	rozkład jazdy/bilet [roskvad yasdeh/bilyet]
train/track	pociąg/tor [posiyong/tor]
platform	peron [peron]
I would like to rent ...	Chciałbym/Chciałabym wynająć ... [Chaubim/Chauabim vinayonts ...]
a car/a bicycle	samochód/rower [sammachod/rover]
petrol/gas station	stacja benzynowa [statsya bensinova]
petrol (gas)/diesel	benzyna/ropy [bensina/roppi]
breakdown/	awaria [avahrya]/
repair shop	warsztat [varshtatt]

FOOD & DRINK

Could you please book a table for tonight for four?	Proszę zarezerwować dla nas na dziś wieczór jeden stolik dla czterech osób [Proshen sareservovatsch dla nas na dsish vechor stollik na tchteri ossobbi]
The menu, please	Czy mogę prosić kartę? [tchi moschay prossits kartenn?]
Could I please have ...?	Chciałbym/chciałabym ...? [Chaubim/chauabim?]
vegetarian/ allergy	wegetarianin/wegetarianka [vegetarianin/ vegetariyanka]/alergia [allergiya]
May I have the bill, please	Proszę o rachunek! [Proshen o rachunek!]

SHOPPING

Where can I find ...?	Przepraszam, gdzie jest ...? [Psheprasham, gsay yest,...?]
I'd like .../ I'm looking for ...	Chciałbym/Chciałabym ... [Chaubim/Chauabim ...]
pharmacy/chemist	apteka/drogeria [aptyeka/drogeriya]
shopping centre	centrum handlowe [sentrum handloveh]
kiosk	kiosk [kiosk]
expensive/cheap/price	drogo/tanio/cena [droga/tannio/tsyena]
more/less	więcej/mniej [viyensay/mninyey]
organically grown	produkt ekologiczny [pradukt ekologitchni]

ACCOMMODATION

I have booked a room	Zarezerwowałem/zarezerwowałam pokój [Sareservovavmem/Saraservovavam pokui]
Do you have any ... left?	Czy ma pan/pani jeszcze ...? [Chi ma pan/panyi yestchyey ...?]
single room	pokój jednoosobowy [pockui yednossobovi]
double room	pokój dwuosobowy [pockui dvosobovi]
breakfast/ half board	ze śniadaniem/ze śniadaniem i kolacją [se shnyadanyam /se shnyadanyam i kollatsiya]
full board (American plan)	z pełnym wyżywieniem [s poynim visiviyeniem]
at the front	od frontu [odd frontu]
shower/sit-down bath	prysznic/łazienka [prichnyits/wasyenka]
balcony/terrace	balkon/taras [balkon/taras]
key/room card	klucz/karta [klootch/karta]
luggage/suitcase/bag	bagaż/walizka/torba [bagasch/valiska/torba]

BANKS, MONEY & CREDIT CARDS

bank/ATM	bank/bankomat [bank/bankomat]
pin code	kod PIN [kod PIN]

I'd like to change ...	Chciałbym/Chciałabym wymienić ... [Chaubim/Chauabim vimenyitch ...]
cash/credit card	gotówka/karta kredytowa [gatuvka/karta kreditova]
bill/coin	banknot/moneta [banknott/moneta]

HEALTH

doctor/dentist/ paediatrician	lekarz/dentysta/pediatra [läkasch/dentista/pädiatra]
hospital/emergency clinic	szpital/pogotowie [schpital/pogotowwijä]
fever/pain	gorączka/ból [gorontschka/bul]
diarrhoea/nausea	rozwolnienie/nudności [roswolniäniä/nudnusjzi]
pain reliever/tablet	środek przeciwbólowy/tabletka [sroddeck pschäziwbulowi/tablättka]

POST, TELECOMMUNICATIONS & MEDIA

stamp/ lettre	znaczek pocztowy [snatchek potchtovi]/ list [list]
postcard	pocztówka [potchtoovka]
I need a landline phone card	Potrzebna mi karta telefoniczna do telefonu domowego [Potchebna mi karta telefonitshna do telefonu domovyeygo]
I'm looking for a prepaid card for my mobile	Szukam karty startowej do telefonu komórkowego [shukam karti startovay do telefonu komurkovego]
Where can I find internet access?	Gdzie znajdę dojście do internetu? [Gsay snidyen doysiya do internetu?]
socket/charger	kontakt/ładowarka [kontakt/wadovarka]
computer/battery	computer/bateria [komputer/bateriya]
internet connection/ wifi	dojście do internetu [doysiya do internetu]/ bezprzewodowy dostęp do internetu [byespshevodovi dosten do internetu]

NUMBERS

0	zero [sero]	10	dziesięć [dyeshentsh]
1	jeden [yeyden]	11	jedenaście [jedenashtya]
2	dwa [dva]	12	dwanaście [dvanashtya]
3	trzy [tshi]	20	dwadzieścia [dvadshastya]
4	cztery [chteri]	50	pięćdziesiąt [pyendyisont]
5	pięć [pyench]	70	siedemdziesiąt [schedemmdyisont]
6	sześć [shesht]	100	sto [sto]
7	siedem [shedemm]	1000	tysiąc [tishonts]
8	osiem [oshemm]	½	jedna druga [jedna druga]
9	dziewięć [djeventsh]	¼	jedna czwarta [jedna tchvarta]

NOTES

MARCO POLO TRAVEL GUIDES

- PACKED WITH INSIDER TIPS
- BEST WALKS AND TOURS
- FULL-COLOUR PULL-OUT MAP
  AND STREET ATLAS

STREET ATLAS

The green line ▬▬▬ indicates the Walking tours (p. 82–87)

All tours are also marked on the pull-out map

Photo: Jagiellonian University

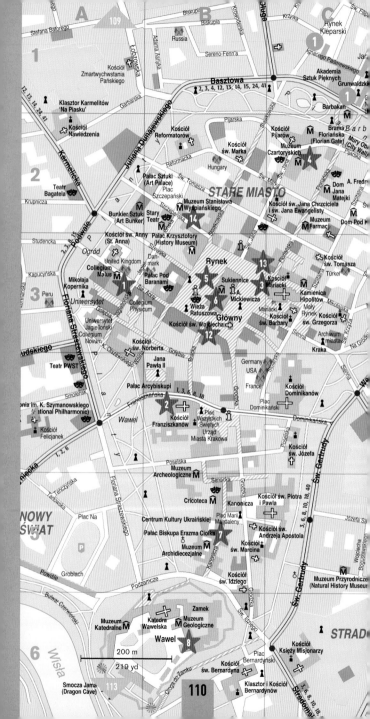

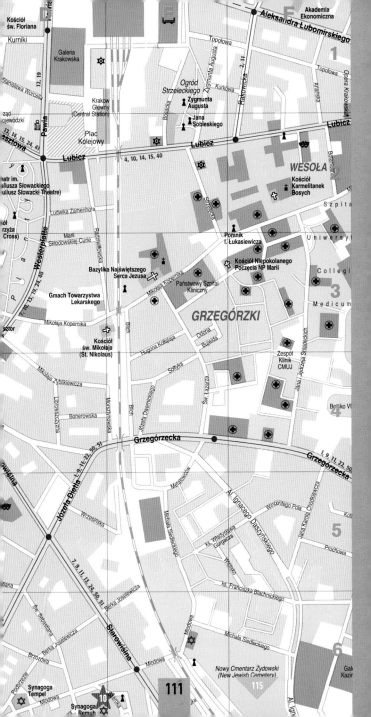

1

Kałuży

Łowiecka

Salwatorska

Łowiecka

Zbigniewa Dunin-Wąsowicza

Kornela Ujejskiego

Syrokomli

Smoleń

Retoryka

Teatr STU

Al. Zygmunta Krasińskiego

Morawskiego

Wóczków

SDT "Jubilat"

Plac
Kossaka

2

Filarecka

Senatorska

pl.
Na Stawach

Marcina (Lelewela) Borełowskiego

Michała Stachowicza

Tatarska

ZWIERZYNIEC

B. Komorowskiego

2

Tadeusza Kościuszki

Bulwar Rodła

Wisła

Most Dębnicki

Bulwa

1, 2, 6

Jaskółcza

3

Madalińskiego

♀

Powroźnicz

Barska

Tyniecka

Rynek
Dębnicki

Różana

Tyniecka

Tyniecka

Skwerowa

Kazimierza Pułaskiego

4

Czecho słowacka

Praska

Zagrody

Michała Bałuckiego

Edmunda Wasilewskiego

Biała Droga

Zagrody

Kościół
św. Stanisława
Kostki

✠

Jaworowa

Dębnicka

Szwedzka

Rolna

Michała Bałuckiego

Konfederacka

Skwerowa

5

DĘBNIKI

Ogródków
Poczty
Gdańskiej

Dębowa

18, 19, 22

Monte

A. Nowaczyńskiego

Dębowa

6

Monte Cassino

Skwedzka

Władysława Miłkowskiego

Mieszczańska

Twardowskie

Zielna

Dworska

skiego

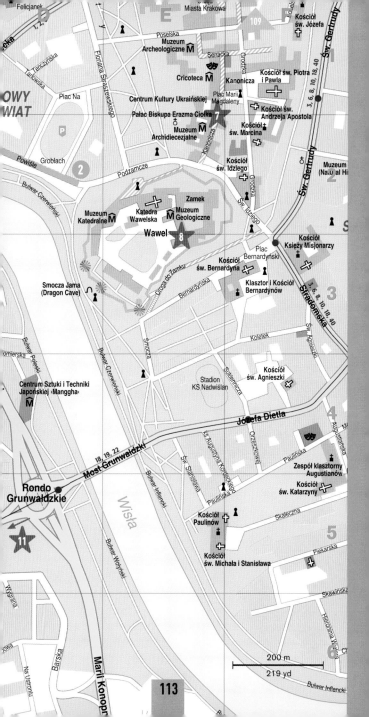

Felicjanek

Miasta Krakowa

Kościół
św. Józefa

Poselska
Muzeum
Archeologiczne Ⓜ

Senacka

Grodzka

Kościół św. Piotra
i Pawła

Cricoteca Ⓜ

Kanonicza

Plac Marii
Magdaleny

Kościół św.
Andrzeja Apostoła

Centrum Kultury Ukraińskiej

Pałac Biskupa Erazma Ciołka

Kościół
św. Marcina

Muzeum
Archidiecezjalne Ⓜ

Kościół
św. Idzlego

Muzeum
(Na...al Hi

Podzamcze

Zamek

Muzeum
Katedralne Ⓜ

Katedra
Wawelska

Muzeum
Geologiczne Ⓜ

Wawel ⑧

Kościół
Księży Misjonarzy

Plac
Bernardyński

Kościół
św. Bernardyna

Smocza Jama
(Dragon Cave)

Droga do Zamku

Klasztor i Kościół
Bernardynów

Bernardyńska

Koletek

św. Agnieszki

Kościół
św. Agnieszki

Centrum Sztuki i Techniki
Japońskiej ›Manggha‹
Ⓜ

Smocza

Stadion
KS Nadwiślan

Sukiennicza

Józefa Dietla

18, 19, 22

Most Grunwaldzki

ks. Augustyna Kordeckiego

Orzeszkowej

Paulińska

Zespół klasztorny
Augustianów

Kościół
św. Katarzyny

Rondo
Grunwaldzkie

Wisła

św. Stanisława

Paulińska

Skałeczna

Kościół
Paulinów

Kościół
św. Michała i Stanisława

Piekarska

Skawińska

Bulwar Wołyński

Marii Konop

200 m

219 yd

Bulwar Inflancki

Scena Kameralna

Wrzesińska

Józefa

Michała Siedleckiego

3, 6, 8, 10...

110

Wojciecha Bogusławskiego

Św. Sebastiana

7, 9, 11, 13, 24, 30, 51

Berka Joselewicza

Muzeum Przyrodnicze
(Natural History Museum)

Św. Sebastiana

Starowiślna

Młodowa

Halicka

STRADOM

19, 22

Brzozowa

Podbrzezie

Berka Joselewicza

Rzeszów

Kościół
Księży Misjonarzy

Stradomska

Synagoga
Tempel

Młodowa

Synagoga
Remuh

10

Miodowa

Szeroka

Synagóga
Popper

Św. Agnieszki

Bożego Ciała

Synagoga
Kupa

Jonatana Warszauera

Stary Cmentarz
(Old Cemetery)

Jakuba

Dajwor

3, 6, 8, 10, 18, 40

Plac
Nowy

Estery

Izaaka

Synagoga
Izaaka

Ciemna

Stara Synagoga

Meiselsa

B. Meiselsa

Centrum Kultury
Żydowskiej

Nowa

Synagoga
Wysoka

Plac
Bawół

Bartosza

Warszauera

Kupa

Krakowska

Augustiańska

Bonifraterska

Józefa

KAZIMIERZ

Wąska

Ga
Mu

Paulińska

Józefa

Zespół klasztorny
Kanoników Laterańskich

Św. Wawrzyńca

Zespół klasztorny
Augustianów

Katarzyny

Dom
Norymberski

Kościół
Bożego Ciała

9

Kościół
Św. Katarzyny

Skałeczna

Św. Wawrzyńca

Bożego Ciała

Gazowa

Podgór

3

Węglowa

Plac
Wolnica

Augustiańska

Muzeum
Etnograficzne

Bocheńska

Bonifraterska

Mostowa

Bulwar Kurlandzki

Piekarska

3, 6, 8, 10, 40

Skawińska

Trynitarska

Szpital
E. Biernackiego

Krakowska

Kościół
Bonifratów

Podgórska

Hieronima Wietora

Adama
Chmielowskiego

Podgórska

Muzeum
Tadeusza Kantora

Nadwiślań

Rybaki

Bulwar Inflancki

Mostu Piłsudskiego

3, 6, 8, 10, 40

Kazimierza Brodzińskiego

Staromostowa

Józefińska

3

Wisła

Przy Moście

Celna

Legionów

Bolesława

Rynek
Podgórski

Pomnik
M. Nowackiego

114

Karola Rolowa

Wilga

Mostu Reinhardta

Karola Rolowa

Planty Nowackiego

Włochowska Wandy

Legionów

Rejtana

Bolesława

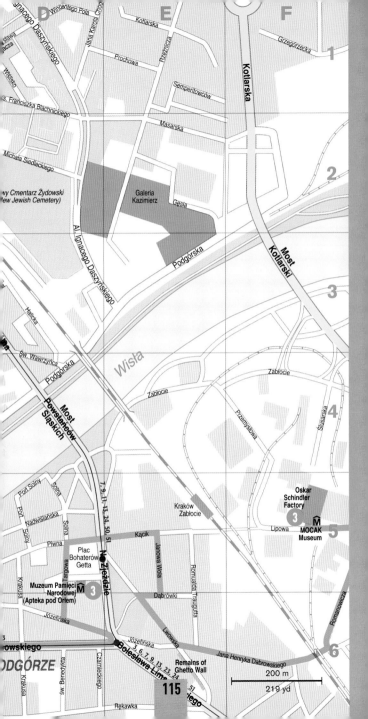

D Wincentego Pola
Jana Karola Chod... E F

Kotlarska

ułnacego Daszyńskiego

sława
acza

Grzegórzecka **1**

Prochowa

Fréżnicza

Wista

Kotlarska

ks. Franciszka Blachnickiego

Semperitowców

Michała Siedleckiego

Masarska

2

wy Cmentarz Żydowski
ew Jewish Cemetery)

Galeria
Kazimierz

Gęsta

Al. Ignacego Daszyńskiego

Podgórska

Most Kotlarski **3**

Herloka

Sw. Wawrzyńca

Podgórska

Wisła

Zabłocie

Zabłocie

Zabłocie

Most Powstańców Śląskich

Przemysłowa

Ślusarska **4**

Port Solny

Solna

Nadwiślańska

Port Solny

Piwna

1, 9, 11, 13, 24, 50, 51

Kraków
Zabłocie

Oskar
Schindler
Factory

Kącik

Janowa Wola

Lipowa

3 Ⓜ MOCAK
Museum **5**

Plac
Bohaterów
Getta

Na Zjeżdzie

Krakusa

Muzeum Pamięci
Narodowej
(Apteka pod Orłem) **3** Ⓜ

Dąbrówki

Romualda Traugutta

Romanowicza

Józefińska

Józefińska

Lwowska

3, 6, 7, 9, 13, 23, 24
51

Jana Henryka Dąbrowskiego **6**

ⓜ

rowskiego

PODGÓRZE

Krakusa

sw. Benedykta

Czarnieckiego

Bolesława Lim...

Remains of
Ghetto Wall

115

200 m

219 yd

Rękawka

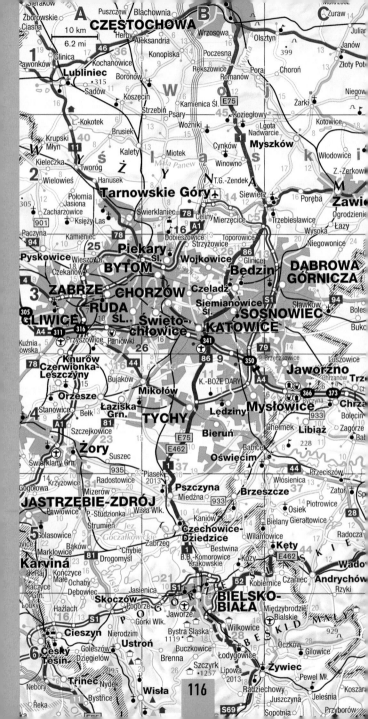

116

This index lists a selection of the streets and squares shown in the street atlas

Ⓜ	Museum
🎭	Stage
ⓘ	Information
✝⛪	Church
⛪	Chapel, monastery
✡	Synagogue
✚	Hospital
✪	Police
🚎	Bus station
♟	Monument
Ⓟ	Parking garage
⛺	Youth Hostel
⚑	Consulate
—●—	Tram with station
▨	Remarkable building
▧	Public building
▢	Green
▢	Uncovered area
▨▨▨	Pedestrian zone
▬▬▬	Walking tours
★ 1	Marco Polo Highlights

INDEX

This index lists all sights, museums, and destinations, plus the names of important people and key words featured in this guide. Numbers in bold indicate a main entry

WRITE TO US

e-mail: info@marcopologuides.co.uk

Did you have a great holiday? Is there something on your mind? Whatever it is, let us know! Whether you want to praise, alert us to errors or give us a personal tip – MARCO POLO would be pleased to hear from you. We do everything we can to provide the very latest information for your trip.

Nevertheless, despite all of our authors' thorough research, errors can creep in. MARCO POLO does not accept any liability for this. Please contact us by e-mail or post.

MARCO POLO Travel Publishing Ltd Pinewood, Chineham Business Park Crockford Lane, Chineham Basingstoke, Hampshire RG24 8AL United Kingdom

PICTURE CREDITS
Cover photograph: St Mary's Church, Rynek Główny (Market Square), getty Images/The Image Bank: Layda
Atelier Femini: Michael Grzywacz (16 centre); R. Freyer (3 centre, 7, 44, 50, 54, 56 left, 66/67, 70, 88, 88/89); getty Images/The Image Bank: Layda (1 top); R. Hackenberg (42); Huber: Gusso (34), Mehlig (18/19), Pavan (35); F. Ihlow (2 centre bottom, 14, 26/27); © iStockphoto.com: 36clicks (17 bottom), Barbara Dudzińska (16 top); La Gioia: Monika Mroczkowska-Biatasik (17 top); Laif: Geilert/Gaff (91), Westrich (front flap left, 10/11); Look: age fotostock (2 centre top, 6, 20, 23, 24 left, 24 right, 86, 92 bottom, 121), The Travel Library (12/13); K. Maeritz (front flap right, 2 bottom, 3 top, 4, 8, 9, 25, 30, 32, 37, 38, 40, 46, 48, 52/53, 59, 60/61, 62, 64, 68/69, 73, 76, 80, 82/83, 84, 87, 89); Massolit Books: Martin Kraft (16 bottom); mauritius images: Alamy (2 top, 3 bottom, 5, 56 right, 74/75, 79, 92 top, 93, 106/107); Transit-Archiv: Hirth (51, 90, 90/91); J. Tumielewicz (1 bottom)

1st Edition 2013
Worldwide Distribution: Marco Polo Travel Publishing Ltd, Pinewood, Chineham Business Park, Crockford Lane, Basingstoke, Hampshire RG24 8AL, United Kingdom. Email: sales@marcopolouk.com
© MAIRDUMONT GmbH & Co. KG, Ostfildern
Chief editor: Marion Zorn
Author: Joanna Tumielewicz, editor: Jens Bey
Programme supervision: Anita Dahlinger, Ann-Katrin Kutzner, Nikolai Michaelis
Picture editor: Gabriele Forst
What's hot: wunder media, Munich
Cartography street atlas & pull-out map: DuMont Reisekartografie, Fürstenfeldbruck; © MAIRDUMONT, Ostfildern
Design: milchhof : atelier, Berlin; Front cover, pull-out map cover, page 1: factor product munich
Translated from German by Robert Scott McInnes; editor of the English edition: Sarah Trenker
Prepress: M. Feuerstein, Wigel
Phrase book in cooperation with Ernst Klett Sprachen GmbH, Stuttgart, Editorial by Pons Wörterbücher

DOS & DON'TS

A few things you should bear in mind in Krakow

DON'T DRINK ALCOHOL IN PUBLIC OR LITTER THE STREETS

In Poland, it is forbidden to drink alcohol in public and to smoke at public transport stops. Krakow is a clean city and there are rubbish bins on every corner. You will be fined if you are caught throwing away a cigarette butt.

DON'T PARK ILLEGALLY

Krakow is divided into three parking zones and you can only park in Zones B and C if you have a valid parking ticket. If you park your car illegally or without a ticket a wheel clamp will make it impossible for you to drive away – and it will be very expensive to have it removed!

DON'T EXCHANGE MONEY AT THE AIRPORT

The exchange rate at the airport is usually the worst in Krakow; compare the rates in the exchange offices in the city. The rate is usually a few *złoty* lower in Sundays.

DON'T GO INTO A CHURCH INAPPROPRIATELY DRESSED

Being a tourist is no excuse for not observing the rule of not wearing shorts or sleeveless garments when you visit a church. You will either not be allowed to enter or asked to put something on. Some churches, such as St Mary's, will provide you with a shawl. Don't forget to take off your headgear!

DON'T BE CARELESS

Krakow is a safe city but you should still not leave any valuables in your car or your camera on a table in a café. The better hotels have safes for your use.

DON'T GRIPE

The Krakowers know that things are still not perfect, that the roads could be better, that the pavements need to be repaired and that more cycle paths would be good. The Poles like to grouse themselves but do not take kindly to criticism from foreigners. Concentrate on all the positive things you experience.

DON'T CROSS THE ROAD WITHOUT LOOKING

You should always look to the left and right a few times even if you are at a zebra crossing or traffic light. Drivers do not always stop even if there is a pedestrian by the roadside. Of course, it is compulsory to stop in Poland – but it does not happen very often!

DON'T MAKE JOKES ABOUT THE CHURCH

98 percent of the Poles are Roman Catholic and the church still plays a major role in society. Therefore: even if the locals make jokes about priests and the church, you should resist any temptation to do the same